JESus

THE PARABLE
OF GOD

*What Do We Really Know
About Jesus?*

EDUARD SCHWEIZER

T&T CLARK
EDINBURGH

Originally published in the United States of America by
Pickwick Publications
4137 Timberlane Drive
Alison Park, PA 15101–2932

This edition published under licence from Pickwick Publications by
T&T CLARK LTD
59 GEORGE STREET
EDINBURGH EH2 2LQ
SCOTLAND

First published 1997

ISBN 0 567 08585 6

British Library Cataloguing-in-Publication Data
A catalogue record for this book is available from the British Library

Printed and bound in Great Britain by Page Bros, Norwich

CONTENTS

PREFACE

This book was not planned. When Dikran Y. Hadidian of Pickwick Publications asked me in 1993 whether I might be able to pen a small monograph on the historical Jesus, I replied that I would probably have neither the strength nor the time for such a task—and that, anyway, the output of theological books was so enormous today that it would rather be an act of grace not to write one more. Yet here is this book. It owes its existence to a string of lucky events (lucky for me, mind you!—whether also for its readers I do not know).

It started with a friendly invitation by Dr. Allen Churchill to come over for three days in September 1992 to deliver the Dominion-Chambers lectures in Ottawa, Ontario on Life-of-Jesus research. So the theme was given to me already in 1992. This was followed the next year by the invitation to give the James D. Belote Memorial lectures on the same general topic at the Hong Kong Baptist Theological Seminary in the first days of 1994 (to be published in Chinese). At both places I have been stimulated and inspired by many discussions in a warm and open atmosphere. Between these two events, I lectured for a week in Nassau Presbyterian Church, Princeton, New Jersey. A member of that church spontaneously gave me a copy of J. D. Crossan's book, a gift that made me read it thoroughly and struggle with its challenge before preparing my Hong Kong lectures—a carbon copy of which I sent to Mr. Hadidian without any thought of publication. After returning from Hong Kong, I was asked by Dr. Amberg of the *Theologische Literaturzeitung* to review G. Lüdemann's very critical and much debated monograph on the resurrection of

Jesus, which made it impossible to avoid tackling the hypothesis that the resurrection of Jesus was merely an intrapsychic hallucination of the disciples. So three invitations to lecture and two gifts of challenging books led me to rethink more and more the question as to who Jesus was (and is!).

The decisive event happened on my eighty-first birthday. I found in my mail the proofs of my Hong Kong lectures, sent by Mr. Hadidian. On the one hand, this was certainly a very welcome present; on the other, it forced me to do what I had not wanted to do—to rewrite almost everything and to expand the original lectures considerably, yet still without knowing when and how I could manage the retyping involved. Then when preaching at the Graduation Service of the Baptist Theological Seminary in Rüschlikon, Zürich, I met my colleague Keith Dyer, professor of New Testament there, and he offered—again spontaneously—to go through my manuscripts, smoothing my English style. With the help of Ms. Clare Hutt, a student of his on exchange from Aberdeen, it was possible to bring together the various layers of original manuscripts, publisher's proofs and all my corrections and elaborations to form a readable and printable computer script. This was a great help and a final liberation from all my worries.

So I am grateful to God for this challenge and opportunity, and I would also like to express my warm thanks to all who helped me so much. First, to those who invited me to lecture: Dr. Churchill in Ottawa, our good friends Dr. and Mrs. W. Alston and Cindy Jarvis in Princeton (not forgetting Mr. and Mrs. Walker and their gift), and the faculty of the Hong Kong Seminary (including a friend of many years, Dr. John Chow, professor of New Testament there). Then my thanks go to all the academic and non-academic participants who listened graciously to me and who helped by their contributions to many discussions, and to Dr. Dyer and Ms. Hutt for their very kind help. Finally, last but not least, I express my deep gratitude to Mr. Hadidian, who urged me to work hard and who was ready to publish the result.

Something of the reality of the Christian Church manifests itself in simple experiences of togetherness. First of all, in the togetherness with Elizabeth in all the ups and downs of a married life of 54 years—and with our children, grandchildren and great-grandchildren—and then also with many friends like those mentioned above. The older I grow, the more important this becomes.

Zürich, June 1994 Eduard Schweizer

I

WHERE ARE WE TODAY IN THE LIFE-OF-JESUS RESEARCH?*

This question is, of course, a question arising out of the historical-critical approach to exegesis. Is it an improper question for those who believe in the risen Christ? I try to live as such a believer myself. Thus I agree with those who declare that the authority of the words given by the risen Christ to his disciples after Easter is not inferior to the words of the earthly Jesus. Though I am convinced that Jesus in his earthly ministry did not speak in the post-Easter language with which John reports his words—a language totally different from what we read in the first three gospels—I think that John has in some passages understood and formulated what Jesus really meant better than the synoptic authors.[1] Moreover, we find in all the gospels the echo of people who have been conquered by Jesus to become his witnesses too. Their books are no mere historical documents, but rather a testimony of faith. Even the selection of sayings and stories to be included in each gospel is always a personal decision and therefore an expression of faith on the part of the author.

---

* A preliminary draft of this chapter has been published in *Festschrift Günter Wagner*, ed. Faculty of the Baptist Theological Seminary (Rüschlikon near Zürich), Berne: Peter Lang, 1994. 157-167. (Abbreviations used are as in: S. Schwertner, *International Glossary of Abbreviations for Theology and Related Subjects*. Berlin/New York: de Gruyter. 1974, reprinted in *Theologische Realenzyklopädie*, same publisher, 1976, 1ff. 345ff., cf. XV-XVI.)

Nonetheless, it *is* important to differentiate between the words (or stories) of the earthly Jesus (as far as we can recognize them) and the ones that originated after Easter.

This is not, in my view, a question of determining major or minor authority. Rather, it is a way of helping our understanding of the text. For we fully understand a statement (or a happening) only when we see in which situation it was reported. What caused the author to include it in the book and what was his purpose? Why did he or she place it in this context, formulate it in this way or even create it (under the influence of his or her Lord)? Such analytical lines of inquiry as these—which aim at seeing something of the development of the Biblical message and at understanding which questions were answered and what insights and situations they were aimed at—are an important part of reading and interpreting the text.

But we must also be aware of the limits of our research. To be sure, the risen Lord is still speaking, but what he says today always has to be checked over against the very earliest documents that were accepted and handed down by the church. The question must be asked whether any new word received today is in line with the fundamental message that was granted to his first disciples. Otherwise we could never distinguish his words from our own words. This shows that the historical-critical method alone will certainly not lead to faith, but it might help to keep faith from becoming superstition.

Thus it makes sense to ask again where we can find our position in the spectrum of modern "life-of-Jesus-research." This is a wider formulation than "research of the historical Jesus." The latter term means, strictly speaking, "the Jesus whom we can 'recover' and examine by using the scientific tools of modern historical research."[2] The "real Jesus" was of course much more than that, just as, for instance, my mother was much more than what could be detected by such tools. Any historian has to "fill out" the facts of which he or she is sure to make a convincing portrait of a living person. As long as he or she is doing so in "honest objectivity", necessarily personally engaged, but cautioning himself or herself against all presuppositions of sympathy or antipathy to the subject of his or her work, this is a fruitful and unavoidable part of the work. In this sense then, we will try to see what modern research has to say to us.

1. A Living Christ without a life of Jesus?

As early as 1906 ALBERT SCHWEITZER showed that a life of Jesus, in the usual sense of the word, could no longer be reconstructed. There is almost nothing to learn about his family, his inner and outer development, the teachers, parents and friends that influenced him, and so on. He concluded that the evangelists are not primarily interested in a historically accurate report, but rather in the proclamation of their faith in Jesus.[3] RUDOLF BULTMANN accepted this result without any reserve. If it is the faith of the early church that is proclaimed even in the gospels, then it is this faith, grounded on the Easter event, that we have to start from. Thus, "Jesus has risen into (not: in!) the kerygma."[4] What he means is the fact that we find Jesus after Easter only in the preaching of the church and that it is only this preaching that understands Jesus correctly. This is undoubtedly true for all believers. Bultmann would even admit that there is something like an implicit christology in the ministry of Jesus. This means that Jesus in his words and deeds claimed to be the definitive revelation of God. Yet whether this was so or not, and in what way he may have claimed to be that, is theologically not decisive for Bultmann. Our faith does not depend on the facts of the life of Jesus. To believe does not mean to take this or that fact for granted, it means to be touched in one's innermost self, to see oneself as one is, and to receive justification from God himself, acceptance as God's child, forgiveness of sins and a new life. It means that we no longer find our real lives in our works, in what we perform and accomplish, nor in our belief, in what we accept as a dogmatic statement of the church.We find our lives in their givenness only, in what we receive and accept as a gift from God. Faith is not a matter of sacrificing our intelligence. It is a change of our self-understanding.

Bultmann's solution was fascinating. It gave his students limitless freedom in historical-critical research yet, at the same time, the possibility to accept the confessions of the church about Jesus Christ, the Son of God and redeemer from all sins. Whether Jesus thought of himself as being the messiah and of dying as an atonement for the sins of the world, was irrelevant, since we knew that he*was* the messiah and that his death *brought* about our salvation. Indeed, he freed the world from trusting in their own works or in their religious convictions. He enabled the world to accept the grace of God. We needed to know no more than the mere "that" of his existence: namely that Jesus had once lived and had died on the cross.

All this became even clearer in the development of Bultmann's program of "demythologization"[5]—of translating all mythical language of times long past into modern, intelligible language. For Bultmann this meant a language dealing with our existence, an existential language. What the Bible describes as the fight of God against Satan or of the spirit against the flesh, modern language describes as the almost ineradicable human desire to "boast", to prove ourselves superior to others, physically or psychically, in terms of wealth or art or even religion. This can only be overcome by the acceptance of the grace of God, by the insight that all we can accomplish is *given* to us. It is the battle in ourselves that really matters.

Even as a student in Marburg, I had asked Bultmann why then did we need Jesus. Was he simply the motivation that led us to accept the same philosophy that he was living from? Would it not be enough just to take over this view of ourselves from the gospels, from Paul or from modern philosophers? Why do we have any need to know more about Jesus, when we can take over the philosophy of Plato without knowing anything about the life and death of Plato? When Bultmann spoke of demythologization, a number of theologians then asked: Why stop at demythologizing Jesus? Should we not also translate the term "God" into modern language and speak of our innermost self, which teaches us to understand life as a gift?[6]

2. The relevance of history

In a famous paper that he read in 1953 in the circle of the Bultmannians, ERNST KÄSEMANN set up the battle cry.[7] The vulnerable spot in Bultmann's position was obviously his difficulty to show why and how Jesus was more than a teacher, or an example, or a model of the insight that life is primarily a gift and not based on our achievements. If salvation means no more than a change in our selfunderstanding (in the terms of Bultmann) or our conversion (in the terms of the traditional church), then we believe actually in our own believing, we trust in our own trusting. Then salvation is reduced to an idea! An idea which reigns over our lives, but which also participates in all the ups and downs of our devotion to that idea. But the Bible proclaims the good deeds of God, which are unconditioned by our behavior and attitude. The gospels are narratives, not abstract philosophies, and the same is true of most parts of the Old Testament.They tell of God's acts, by which the people of God have been guided, and of Jesus, the one in whom God came to us and by whom we have been reconciled and made to be God's children. This has happened long before we did anything for God and it was pure grace that no human philosophy could have expected. God acted "outside of us," as the Reformers said.

In many ways, one could bypass the problem. In 1959 JAMES ROBINSON spoke of *A New Quest of the*

Historical Jesus,[8] stressing both sides of the truth: the gospels are not biographies but rather sermons proclaiming the grace of God, a grace that has become true in an earthly life and death which can be dated within the history and geography of our world. Thus, what we find in the gospels is the faith of the four evangelists, a faith shaped by the whole ministry of Jesus, including his death. This faith certainly presupposes the resurrection, which is important to the authors of the gospels, but more important for Robinson as God's vindication of the *earthly* ministry of Jesus. Thus the Gospels provide the narrative of a human life and death in which we find the revelation of God.

Does this mean that we could do without the resurrection of Jesus? This seems to be so with HERBERT BRAUN.[9] He restored Bultmann's view (and Bultmann accepted it) but founded it on the ministry of Jesus, not on the faith of the post-Easter church. It is, according to him, the earthly Jesus who liberated his hearers to be able to see themselves as loved and accepted by God and, therefore, also to be able to love others. The resurrection added nothing to this central new understanding of oneself. Braun even argued that the continuity underlying the whole New Testament was provided precisely by this new understanding of humanity (anthropology), not by the understanding of Jesus as Christ (christology). Even God seemed to disappear: according to Braun, seeing one's brother is seeing God.[10]

In 1967 DOROTHEE SÖLLE did replace God by Jesus. What God used to be for people, Jesus is now, because God is dead. Therefore, for Sölle, the resurrection is better understood as a newly reached oneness and identity for all people. In a society without class distinctions, God might come alive again.[11] She certainly said these things against a very conservative position, in which God had become a mere object, the existence of which one simply had to take for granted without really getting engaged with his or her total existence. I know few theologians who try to think and to speak as seriously and honestly as Braun and Sölle. For both, Jesus is central, though for them he teaches and lives in a way that, in principle, every human being could be capable of. Nonetheless, isn't their Jesus—without God as his father and Lord—rather like an ambassador who still holds his office, though his country has ceased to exist long ago?

Also remarkable is the recent trend to place Jesus—and to some degree also the earliest church—back into the context of Judaism. This trend has been especially significant since the publication of E.P.SANDERS' books at the end of the seventies.[12] It focuses, like Braun and Sölle, on the earthly ministry of Jesus of Nazareth rather than emphasizing his resurrection and his role in the post-Easter church. But in contrast to them, the uniqueness of this earthly ministry is rather toned down. Jewish authors—and those in dialogue with Judaism—"reclaim" Jesus for Judaism and try to bring him home to Israel.

Undoubtedly Jesus was a Jew and this is important. The same is true for most of the authors of the New Testament and this is also important. One of the principal difficulties in the dialogue between Jews and Christians and in the contemporary approach to belief in Jesus Christ, is the fact that we think in terms of "substance", a tendency which we inherited from the Greeks and especially from Aristotle. This way of thinking has become, if not wrong, at least questionable today. In modern natural science everything is understood in terms of motion and energy so that terms like "matter" are no longer used without qualification. Even in Jerusalem at the time of Jesus, Hellenistic views had prevailed for almost three centuries and Greek was spoken by many Jews there, and perhaps even by Jesus—though it remains improbable that any of his words reported in the gospels were originally in Greek.[13] Yet in areas in which the Hebrew Bible was of first importance—and this includes the whole sphere of religious life—its way of thinking clearly influenced basic understandings. When a Jewish Christian confessed Jesus as the son of God, he did so in the way his Bible taught him. The king became son of God when he acceded to the throne of Israel (Ps 2:7). From then on it was God who acted and who spoke through him. Thus the title "son of God" qualified in a dynamic—not a static—way, his life as the representative of God, and not his "nature" as such. We certainly have to understand the message of Jesus and of the New Testament in this way. Whenever we speak of a living being, we do not define it only in a "static" way, rather we have to *tell* people about it. If you ask me who my wife is, you don't expect an answer in terms of measurements of weight and height: rather I must tell you where she was born, what her vocation was, how she brought up our children, and so on. In the same way it is impossible to give a definition of God or of Jesus. That he is the son of God does not mean that his body is of a different substance from our bodies. It means that in his life, his death and his resurrection, God himself spoke, lived, and acted with and for us. If we understand our confession in this sense, a contemporary Jew would at least understand what we want to say. In a similar way it is true of many statements in our "New" Testament that they are only understandable in the context of their Jewish, and that means basically "Old" Testament, background.

3. *The Specific Status of Jesus within this Jewish Context*

As a Christian I would not be taking my Jewish partner in dialogue seriously[14] if I did not add that for me, Jesus is also the son of God in an "eschatological way." This is to say that he is the fulfillment of all the kings and righteous ones—or even of the whole people of Israel—who could be named son of God in the Hebrew Bible. And for me he is this in a unique way, not simply more of a son of God than David or any righteous Jew. That Jesus is a

Jew and that we have to understand what it means when we call him son of God is clear, and here Jews and Christians would agree. Can we say more than that?

According to MAURICE CASEY[15] Jesus was a Jewish prophet, who never used any title like messiah, son of God or lord as a self-identification, who humbly spoke of himself, sometimes using the phrase "son of man" in a very general sense, more or less as we use "one." He expected the imminent end of the world and the final coming of the kingdom of God. Therefore he intensified the commands of the Mosaic law, with an emphasis on the love of one's neighbor. With regard to himself, he expected his death and his vindication by God. Since, however, his disciples and all those who shared their beliefs had to find their identity after Easter over against the Jews that did not accept those beliefs, they needed a miracle like Jesus' exaltation to heaven (as happened to Enoch and Elijah according to the scriptures) and a new focus for their faith: Jesus instead of the law. It was not yet Paul, but John, who went so far as to call Jesus "God," and this confession then remained the position of the church from the council of Chalcedon on.

Equally radical and probably of wider influence, is JOHN DOMINIC CROSSAN'S *The Historical Jesus*.[16] The first half of the book is a most interesting description of the world in which Jesus was living. The author shows an astonishingly wide knowledge of the work done by historians and especially sociologists, from which we can learn much. In the second half he deals with the problem of the historical Jesus, as we find him in the literary sources. In Crossan's view "magic" and "meals" were central for Jesus and his movement, that is to say: healings and eating in an egalitarian community formed the basis for the Jesus movement. The background is the situation of the poor peasants and small craftsmen. The kingdom of God is a present, not a future reality. Jesus may have shared at first

some apocalyptic hopes with John the Baptist, but gave
them up when he severed himself from John. For Crossan,
the calling of the disciples by Jesus to follow him is not authentic,[17] nor is the phrase "son of man" as referring to Jesus himself,[18] the "our Father"-prayer[19] or the parable of the
prodigal son.[20] The parables tell of common sense decisions. Of course one chooses the good fish, not the bad and
sometimes one sheep may become more important than
ninety-nine.[21] Jesus is a charismatic leader, challenging all
hierarchical structures, not interested in any institutionaliza-
tion of his group, fighting against the wealth and power of
the temple and therefore finally crucified without a trial be-
forehand or an orderly burial afterwards.[22] The stories of
his appearances as the risen lord to his disciples as well as
the list of them in 1 Cor 15:5-8 mirror post-Easter fights for
power among the leaders of the early church.[23] Methodo-
logically, Crossan starts from the criterion of multiple attestation. Only sayings or stories that are reported in two or
more sources independent of one another are a safe foundation for any reconstruction of the life of Jesus. In doing this
he is not concerned "with an unattainable objectivity, but
with an attainable honesty," a position with which you can
but sympathize,[24] a position which seems to be unchal-
lengeable.

4. *Critical Questions*

Yet there are difficulties. *First*, there is the problem
of dating the sources. Which one testifies to an early, which
to a later stratum of tradition? There might be early traditions in texts that are rather late and vice versa. Is a clear
development discernible from one position to another one
and in which direction does it move? Admittedly the two-
source-hypothesis—that Matthew and Luke knew Mark
and a collection of sayings and of a few stories of Jesus
(Q)—is very probably correct. But what about the Gospel
of Thomas, which certainly contains strange gnostic passages that seem to be of rather late origin? Whether or not

there are any texts of an earlier date than our gospels, is very much disputed. We possess the Gospel of Thomas in a Coptic translation, found at Nag Hammadi and rather difficult to date.[25] Many scholars conclude that it is dependent on our canonical gospels. The same is true of the Gospel of Peter,[26] which we know from a manuscript of the 8th or 9th century, found in Egypt. It is very doubtful whether we could still reconstruct out of it what Crossan calls a "Cross gospel" that would give us an earlier layer of the passion story.[27] Even more questionable is "The Secret Gospel of Mark," quoted only around 200 by Clement of Alexandria in a letter of which we have a copy (or rather the photograph of it) written around 1750.[28] Finally, there is the letter of Barnabas written probably between 90 and 135.[29] It is an allegorizing interpretation of many passages of the Hebrew Bible.

Second, Crossan speaks of an earlier and a later stratum in Q. But there are no objective criteria to distinguish between them or, more significantly, to justify putting them into a chronological order. Even more central is the question whether Q was ever the only gospel of a congregation. Perhaps it was a collection of sayings of Jesus in a church that celebrated the passion and the resurrection in its liturgy and/or read the story of Good Friday and Easter in an early gospel. Q might even have been used from its beginning in the same church together with the Gospel of Mark, as we use booklets with selected Biblical words for married couples or a digest of ethical advice from Thomas a Kempis beside our Bible. I do not believe in the hypothesis of a plurality of different early churches with different gospels. There were certainly various and different strands of tradition, but Paul, whose conversion must have taken place within one to three years after the death of Jesus and who lived and worked outside of Jerusalem and Judaea (in places where the so called Hellenistic Jews were living), knows of only one early church in which there were different views, for instance, of gentile mission (Gal 1:17-24; 2:1-2). One might also compare the Johannine literature.

The letters never mention an earthly ministry of Jesus, and yet they presuppose the gospel of John. Therefore, it is very uncertain whether there ever existed a congregation for which the cross and the resurrection were of no importance.[30]

  Third, to be sure, there are processes of development in the tradition, but it is not easy to say which was the earlier and which was the later stage. Is the more complex form an expansion of the simpler one or is the latter an extract from the former? Take, for instance, the story of Secret Mark about Jesus in Bethany: A woman, rebuked by the disciples, asks Jesus: "Son of David, have mercy upon me," and goes with him into the garden. A great cry is heard from a tomb. Jesus rolls the stone away, raises a rich youth and teaches him the mystery of the kingdom of God.[31] This looks to me definitely like a very late, and rather fantastic, combination of the woman in Bethany and the resurrection of Lazarus (John 11:38-12:2; cf. Mark 14:3), of the cry of the blind man in Jericho and the rebuking of the disciples (Mark 10:47; 10:13), of the stone rolled away from the tomb of Jesus (Mark 16:3), of the rich youth (see only Matthew 19:20-22) and the youth with a cloth on his naked body in Gethsemane (Mark 14:51-52) and of the phrase "the mystery [singular] of the kingdom of God"-(Mark 4:11). I really doubt how we could find here some pre-gospel story. I see rather something like that which happened in the clearly late combination of several gospels in the final passage of Mark 16:9-20. The same could be true of the gospel of Thomas. There are many sayings there that combine words of Jesus which are to be found in the canonical gospels (cf. e.g. 21, 47, 76). There are also changes that are, in my view, evidently later interpretations. The lost sheep is important because it is the largest (107, cf. the large good fish in 8). One might add 26, 61, 69, 77, 79, 89, 101, 104, 109. Later expansions do, of course, not disprove the possibility that also very early forms may have been kept, but this is difficult to prove. Other texts contain the Pauline emphasis on the contrast between flesh and spirit (29) or the (apocryphal) word quoted in 1 Cor 2:9 (17). Ideas like that of the world as a corpse (56), or of a primeval human being who was male and female (11, 22, 106), or even a word of Jesus that he would make a woman a male to save her (114), do not seem to stem from Jesus. Nor does the saying about undressing without shame as a means to see the son of God (37), or the polemic against three gods instead of one or two (30).

Fourth, on the one hand, it goes without saying that terms or ideas that are no longer important in the post-Easter church may easily be dropped in its documents. Thus, double attestation is not to be expected. For instance, Didache 16:6-8 and Apocalypsis Eliae 32:4 (JSHRZ V/3, p. 251 with note d) contain an expanded and theologically developed form of the prophecy of the "sign of the son of man," the "trumpet call" and the vision of the "son of man coming on the clouds of heaven" (Matt 24:30-31), but without the double mention of the "son of man." It is not impossible that this goes back to a pre-Matthean form without that term, but more probably, it is a reference to Matthew without the obsolete term of "son of man". On the other hand, it is to be expected that terms or ideas important for the church will be found more than once, even if they originated after Easter. For instance, to *watch* before the last judgment comes (the "thief," not the "Lord"), was an important piece of advice in the early church. Therefore the aphorism of Luke 12:39-40 Q is also to be found in 1 Thess 5:2; 2 Peter 3:10; as a saying of the risen Lord in Rev 3:3 and 16:15 and in the Gospel of Thomas 21:3.[32] This excellent multiple attestation certainly does not prove that it was ever spoken by the earthly Jesus. No doubt it would be desirable to have two or more witnesses to the authenticity of a painting by, let us say Van Gogh, for it is true that after he had created that style of art, some could imitate him. But there would be very, very few that could deceive us if we really love his paintings and have seen them time and time again. In a similar way, there are sayings of Jesus in which his spirit proves itself.

Fifth, my main objection to the reconstruction of Crossan is still another one. If Jesus' earthly ministry had been only what Crossan suggests, who would have created the rest of our Gospels? We would then be forced to assume the existence of quite a number of people who would have sometimes even exceeded the genius of Jesus. Who would have created parables like that of the prodigal son or sayings like the one of the coming lord, serving at the table (Luke 12:37. Cf. 22:27; John 13:1-17)? Or who would have composed scenes like that of Gethsemane or the story of the crucifixion, in which Jesus utters the phrase "My God, my God, why have you forsaken me?" and dies with a loud cry followed by the confession of a gentile officer: "Truly this man was son of God"? Who would have spoken of the coming kingdom without adding apocalyptic details and indicating some date of this event?

There are also questions of historical probabilities (in the narrower sense of the word). Is it probable that John the Baptist focused his preaching on the future and that the earliest church understood in a similar apocalyptic way the resurrection of Jesus, as far as we can see, as the beginning of the end of the world, if Jesus had spoken exclusively of the present kingdom without any emphasis on the fulfillment in the future? And can we really imagine that the last meal of Jesus was nothing more than a normal meal?[33] Paul refers to his tradition of this meal as coming from the lord himself (1 Cor 11:23), and he visited Peter (and James) in Jerusalem for two weeks within the first few years after Jesus' death.[34] Would he never have detected that the history of that last meal had developed only after Easter into a liturgy of the church, which interpreted it by the words of institution? Would he really quote them as the very words of Jesus if they had only originated in the reflections of the church?

5. *Should We Give Up?*

Crossan and I would agree that neither his nor my reconstruction can, in the strict sense of the word, be proven or disproven. There is, indeed, no attainable one hundred percent assurance. Have we therefore come to a blind alley? *Either* we side with Bultmann's original position and decide to accept the faith of the early church as a decision that cannot be argued this way or that way. This leads to the problem of understanding the significance of the role of Jesus—his life, his death and his resurrection. It also means that the real saving event would then simply be a change of mind—or in traditional terms: our innermost conversion—in which Jesus may have helped merely as a teacher and a model. Is this enough? Would we, in this case, not be simply believing in our own believing, and in our own religiosity? And would not our faith or trust in God change with all the ups and downs of our religious feelings and experiences? *Or* we side with Käsemann and many others after him: in which case the difficult problem of the historian faces us. If history is of preeminent importance, who will tell us whether Jesus was a preacher of existentialism, as Braun sees him, or a left wing politician as Sölle or Machovec understood him, or a psychotherapist, as Niederwimmer thinks,[35] or a Jewish prophet as Casey suggests, or a charismatic leader of a peasant movement, as Crossan paints him, or still yet somebody else?

I shall try to answer these questions in three points, which will be taken further in the chapters to follow. First, I certainly side with Käsemann and Karl Barth. In Jesus God brought his history with his people Israel to the goal. This has become true "outside" of our assent and before we knew anything of it. Our salvation is God's doing. Jesus is certainly an example and a model (John 13:15), but he is much more than that (13:8). This "more" is asserted in the New Testament in many images, but they all try to express the truth that salvation has happened there and then, at a

specific place and time within our earthly history. Therefore, honest historical research on the life and death of Jesus is important.

Second, assurance in all details is never possible.
Classical historians sometimes grin at the scruples of the
New Testament colleagues; if they investigated the history
of antiquity as critically as we do, they would find very little. Even in the life of my own mother there are few details
that are beyond all doubt. My sister often tells a story differently from how I remember it. Yet there is an overall
picture of her life which cannot be doubted. I wonder
whether this would not put a question mark behind the pro-
cedures of the Jesus-Seminar in California, where single
words or stories are discussed and voted upon as to whether
they are authentic or not and to what degree of certainty.[36]
Sometimes, one cannot see the forest while simply focus-
sing on this or that tree. There are more criteria for discern-
ing historicity than the one of multiple attestation and we
shall work in the next chapter with some of them.

Third, my main point is the fact that we certainly
cannot assess Jesus separately from the impact he made.
We know him only through those who have been challenged, who have been helped in physical and psychical
difficulties and ailments, who have found a new sense of
life or peace, and whose whole existence has been changed
by Jesus and the proclamation of his disciples. It is impossible to draw an absolutely clear line between the preaching
and life of Jesus and that of his followers. This leads us to
the problem of the canon. The canon has not been created
by more or less haphazard decisions of the church in the
centuries which followed. Decisions of this kind did happen, but they were only of marginal significance. By and
large, the writings that proved their spiritual power during
the first two centuries have been acknowledged. Do we
really know of any other book of that time which we would
want to include in the New Testament? And do we really
want to remove one?[37]

Thus we are faced with the simple alternative, whether we think that the early church was wrong, not only in details, but in its main direction, or whether we think that our New Testament presents, on the whole, a fair image of Jesus' life and death and of the Easter events. This includes the other question we asked, whether or not we believe that the impact Jesus made on his disciples is still (or perhaps even *more*) detectable behind the testimony of authors (like that of the Fourth Gospel) who speak of him in terms of the time after Easter and in relation to problems of that time. If we believe—and this is, of course, a decision of faith—that there was the guidance of God's spirit in that church, then it is no longer necessary to draw an exact line between the earthly Jesus and the impact he made on his followers. We shall certainly ask critically where foreign influences have veiled or even destroyed this impact, but we shall read and listen with a preconceived trust and expecting to learn from authors that speak not with an absolute authority, but with authority nonetheless.

II

JESUS THE PARABLE-TELLER

If it is true that it will not be necessary to draw the line between Jesus himself and the impact he made rigorously, it is also true that we should become aware of—and sensitive to—the development of the tradition from Jesus to the preaching of the church in its post-Easter situation. Faith that loses its roots in the concrete event of the life and death of Jesus of Nazareth (which can be dated chronologically and fixed geographically) becomes ideology. The statement of Paul (2 Cor 12:10): "When I am weak, then I am strong" (which Jesus could have said in a similar way), could be understood as a statement of existential philosophy. Then it might be interpreted to mean that failures may be more helpful than victories, which sometimes proves to be right and sometimes not. With Paul this understanding is the consequence of a story and senseless without that story: Jesus of Nazareth has died on the cross outside of Jerusalem in the year (plus/minus) 30 A.D. and God has revealed to the disciples, including Paul, within a short period after Easter day that this was God's act of salvation. By this act, God has forgiven, accepted and loved all those who are willing to be forgiven, accepted and loved. When we therefore go back to investigate the life and death of Jesus and the Easter events, we shall first rethink what the criteria are for evaluating the authenticity of the tradition, and then deal with the fact (which nobody doubts) that Jesus spoke in parables, illustrating this by a well attested short parable (Luke 13:21).

1. *The Criteria Again*

What are the criteria for evaluating the authenticity of the Jesus tradition? John P. Meier discusses five criteria that are still valid (we follow here his sequence):[38]

1. *"Embarrassment"* : actions or sayings of Jesus that are obviously difficult for the early church—for instance, his baptism by John (which suggests that John is the superior one), or Jesus' ignorance of the day and hour of the parousia (Mk 13:32).

2. *"Discontinuity"* : whatever cannot be explained as originating in Judaism or in the early church probably comes from Jesus. This is a most debated criterion.[39] Clearly, if applied rigorously, it would lead to a minimum of authentic Jesus traditions. For a Jesus who shared nothing with both the Jewish world of which he was a part and the early church which believed in what his own disciples told it, would be a caricature. However, if we bear in mind this qualification, dissimilarity is still a helpful criterion and we shall use it when speaking of the parables of Jesus.

3. *"Multiple attestation"* : we have discussed this in the first chapter (p.13) and provided we remember that double attestation is sometimes no more than an influence of an early source on a later one, or that it might come from common oral tradition or from "church language," it too can be a useful criterion.

4. *"Coherence"* is more important, in my view. Whatever fits well into the minimum resulting from criteria 1-3, may be accepted tentatively as genuine Jesus tradition.

5. *"Rejection"* : Jesus was rejected by many of his contemporaries and finally crucified. Actions and sayings that can satisfactorily explain why this happened, are with some probability historical facts.

Meier then also discussed five more dubious criteria: Aramaisms, Palestinian environment, vividness of narration, contrast to tendencies of the Synoptic authors, and historical presumption.[40] But in this group of criteria little practical help is to be expected. If, however, we find that more than one of the first five criteria applies to a tradition, we may proceed with some confidence. Yet it should be noted that sensitivity is sometimes more important than mere logical procedure, since it helps to build up a consistent overall picture of Jesus, of his preaching and healing and eating with people, as well as of the destiny that finally led him to the cross and to the events after Easter.[41]

2. The Criterion of Dissimilarity: The Parables.

Parables of Jesus are attested in multiple strands of the tradition—in Q, in Mark and in the gospel of Thomas. Nobody doubts that Jesus spoke in parables. But how does the criterion of discontinuity or dissimilarity apply in this case? There are many rabbinical parables handed down to us. Yet years ago, ERNST FUCHS of Marburg, reputedly—according to some credible rumors—declared that the only thing New Testament scholars had found out in the last fifty years was the fact that Jesus had told parables. What did he mean if this was not simply a silly joke? I think that this comment raises a very important point indeed, one of great relevance for the whole problem of the historical Jesus. For there is a decisive difference between the parables of the rabbis and those of Jesus. The former start from a sentence that has to be proven—from a biblical commandment and its interpretation, for instance. Then follows a parable, using imagery to illustrate the point of the sentence, so that people would say: "Of course, so it is!" When the audience has understood this, the parable has done its service and is no longer necessary. One may forget it. I am sure that in the first grade at school my teacher used such imagery when he taught us the letters of the alphabet. He said something like: "Capital F looks like a flag, doesn't

it?" I now know what a capital F looks like, thus I no longer need such images and I have totally forgotten them.
They are now obsolete. But this is obviously not what the
parables of Jesus are like.

Jesus does *not* teach first in plain language what he
wants to bring home to the people, and then illustrate it by
a parable. He starts directly with the story or he introduces
it with a mere "The kingdom of God is like...." Nor do we
find a summary in plain language afterwards. There *are*
some such summaries, but they have very probably been
added by those who handed down the parable or who read
and tried to interpret it. For example, after the parable of
the unjust steward (Luke 16:1-13) there are three or four
different attempts to express the meaning of the parable:
the dishonest servant is shrewd enough to think of what
comes to him after the judgment by his lord, whereas the
sons of the light forget to do so; or—make friends for your-
selves by means of mammon; or—don't be dishonest in
very little things, so that true riches will be entrusted to
you; or—you cannot serve God and mammon. It is quite
clear that with these conclusions the church later on tried to
understand the parable in very different ways. We could
also think of the parable of the unrighteous judge in Luke
18:1-8, which starts: "He told them a parable that they
ought always to pray and not lose heart," and repeats this
advice in other words at the end. But the rarity of these
comments and the awkwardness of these interpretations
that do not really fit the story, show that they are added sec-
ondarily.

Thus a parable of Jesus cannot be reduced to a doctrinal or hortatory statement so that we could dispense with
it and be satisfied that we now know its main point. Something similar is to be found in 2 Sam 12:1-4, in the parable
of the rich man who slaughters the poor man's lamb. There
is no introduction in plain language, and there is only one
final interpretation of the parable (after David had really

got engaged by it!): *"You* are the man!" It contains also very surprising traits in v. 3 (the lamb lies in his bosom like a daughter), as the parables of Jesus do. This parable is no illustration of a general truth either, but a direct word of God into a very specific situation of the hearer. It can only be understood from the inside (like the parables of Jesus) by someone who accepts God's call to him or her through the prophet who speaks in the authority of God.

Obviously it is very important to see not merely what the contents of the parables of Jesus are, but also to ask *why* he spoke in parables. If they are not simply illustrations of some major doctrines or commandments, what are they? This question represents, according to Fuchs, a most important new achievement of New Testament research in our century; for whenever Jesus speaks about his central concern, the mystery of the kingdom of God, he does so almost always more or less parabolically. Why is it that this kingdom can not be proclaimed without the language of parables or the performance of parabolic action?

3. A One-Verse-Parable: Luke 13:21.

As a result of intensive research on this problem of the parables by many of my colleagues,[42] I see five major points which I shall try to illustrate by interpreting the one-verse-parable in Luke 13:21. It belongs to the sayings source Q and is connected there with the parallel parable of the mustard seed, which is also reported by Mark (4:30-32). Whereas Luke has both parables later in his Gospel in chapter 13, obviously following the Q context, Matthew chooses to follow Mark, adding the Q parable of the leaven to that of the mustard seed. This parable of the leaven fulfills the requirements of the following criteria for authenticity: (1. "Embarrassment") "leaven" usually means something like impurity, therefore, (2. "Discontinuity") neither the rabbinical writings nor Philo nor the Greek literature[43] nor the language of the church (1 Cor 5:6-8) would suggest

this parable. (3. "Multiple Attestation") It is reported in Q
and in the Gospel of Thomas (96:1) and (4. "Coherence") is
clearly connected with the parable of the grain of mustard
seed, which is also to be found in Mark 4:31-32. (5. "Rejection") The proclamation of a kingdom which will "leaven
the whole dough" (The Imperium Romanum? the world?)
might well kindle a fire of wrath against Jesus.

Luke 13:21 runs: "The kingdom of God is like leav-
en, which a woman took and hid in three measures of flour,
till it was all leavened." What happens when Jesus tells this
parable? Let us imagine a peasant's wife listening to him.
The *first* thing that strikes her is the short introduction, in
other parables often only implied, which shows that in the
story the very person and rule of God will come to the hearers and that it is only the authority of the speaker, Jesus,
that vouches for the fact: "The kingdom of God is like leav-
en...". Thus the truth of that parable depends on the question whether this Jesus has the power to identify the coming
of the kingdom with his telling that short story. What an
amazing claim, thinks the woman, from an ordinary man
like one of us here! She has been struck by the central message of Jesus, which arouses in her the decisive question
whether or not this claim might be true. This status of Jesus—as the one in whose words God visits the hearers and
tries to enter their everyday lives—lies at the very basis of
all his parables.

Second, ". . . like leaven, which a woman took. . ."
That's what she has done many times, actually just yesterday. Thus the word of Jesus comes into her world and
fetches her where she is really living. She is not supposed
to emigrate into another world, to retreat from the everyday
world into the world of religion. This is what Jülicher[44] and
others have rightly emphasized. But what does this mean?
The woman detects that Jesus does not give her some new
doctrine or commandment. He refers to an experience she
has had yesterday and many times before. She realizes that

this kingdom of God seems to have something to do with her, a peasant's wife, not only with males, not only with scribes, who can read and write and even understand Hebrew. A specific level of intellectual ability does not seem to be a condition for getting involved. The kingdom is coming to her. Thus, she has already understood the most important truth about the parables of Jesus. They can only be understood by someone who lets the parable drag him into the story they tell. They can be understood only from the inside.[45] When a parable reaches out to us to seize us, we have to be prepared to enter into it.

In the story of Jesus there is no new information for her. She knows how to bake bread. The story rather tries to awaken some of the experiences she had when baking bread to lead her to an experience of God coming to her in order to rule her life. Something similar happens whenever we use imagery in our language. We have, by necessity, to get involved ourselves. First, we have to realize that it is imagery and not to be understood in the literal sense. To give a silly example, when an American calls his girl "honey," a machine could not distinguish that from the honey produced by bees and would, for instance, translate literally into German (where it would sound as if he had said "marmalade"). And even if we could construct a computer that could distinguish from the context whether "honey" means this or that, it could not tell us *how* it is said. Whether in the way a sales-girl asks "What can I do for you, honey? (where "honey" means no more than "madam") or in the way a true lover might say it, maybe with all the enthusiasm of an adolescent. So the woman who listens to Jesus has to listen with all her senses and she understands that she herself has come into the midst of this parable. It really is the kingdom of God which approaches her—even such a simple woman in the hills of Galilee.

Third, Jesus speaks of "three measures of flour." This is by no means impossible, but it is amazing for it is

about 50 pounds.[46] The woman may laugh a bit inwardly:
three measures of flour! How should I work with so much
flour on my kitchen table or before my tent? That would re-
quire quite a lot of work and would produce bread for an
enormously long period, so that most of the loaves would
get very hard. But this inward chuckle works on her. She
tries, perhaps, to imagine how she would manage with such
a heap of flour and the more she does so, the more she feels
that Jesus speaks of something which is very mighty, very
big.

Now similar traits to this are to be found in most of
Jesus' parables. They are never speaking of fairy-tale miracles, but they speak of very unexpected, surprising facts.
What money-lender disposes of sixty million—not dollars,
but sixty million times one day's wages—and most surprisingly of all, simply tears up the IOU of his debtor when he
is unable to pay his debts back? (Matt 18:24-27). What
mustard seed grows into a tree? (Luke 13:19). It might become a very big shrub and you might call it a tree, but it
would be an unusual exaggeration. Where in our world are
there kings that invite the poor and maimed people to their
banquets? (Luke 14:21). Or would a farmer, after sowing,
really only "sleep and rise" until the harvest is ready, without fencing in the field or setting up scare-crows? (Mark
4:26-28). And what fathers behave like the father of the
prodigal son? (Luke 15:11-32). I think, in clear contrast to
Crossan,[47] that the parables of Jesus are *not* illustrations
that convince the hearers because they match their common
sense so that they respond: "Of course, that goes without
saying!" On the contrary, the vital and most important part
of Jesus' parables is the uncommon act or event that startles
the hearer.

This becomes very clear in the parable of the prodigal son (see below, pp. 62-66). In a colloquium of profes-
sors of the University of Geneva, which dealt with that story, a psychiatrist[48] showed how the behavior of the two

sons follows exactly the pattern of modern psychological analysis of adolescents, especially the Freudian Oedipus complex. The younger son actually kills his father, since he acts as if the father had already died: "Give me the share of property that belongs to me." In that time and culture, such a request never should have been made before the father had died, but if it were absolutely necessary to do so because the son wished to emigrate for good, he could sell his share only in anticipation of the time after his father's death. The purchaser of the son's share would wait in expectation of possessing that share in a future period of time.[49] The elder son has killed the father, because for a long time he has not loved and served his father, but merely the picture he had of him—the father as he should be in his view. Both sons are portrayed in a pointed way and they challenge us to identify ourselves with them, but the main message of the parable lies in the picture of the father. And this is very, very unusual indeed. Only Jesus who claims to know his father in heaven better than any other human being, can dare to paint this picture of unlimited love. In a similar way, the woman, startled with the unusually big heap of flour, learns that the kingdom of which Jesus tells seems to be something very great and that something very great is happening just now when Jesus tells his story and she listens to it.

Fourth, "...and hid it under...". Maybe the woman was puzzled and immediately wondered why he told it in this way. Perhaps she only remembered it afterwards. It is possible to describe it this way, but everyday language would not use the verb "to hide" when describing the making of bread. One would rather expect the narrator to speak about "mixing" the leaven with the flour. Did Jesus want to say that this great kingdom, big and awe inspiring as it may be, comes at the same time in a hidden way? Again, this awakens memories of her experience. To be sure, when she finished with mixing and kneading the dough, the leaven disappeared. It is totally hidden and yet it is in the dough and it works and lives there. Would the kingdom of God be hidden in this way too? She certainly does not see it or even anything of its effects. The world is every day the same: wars are threatening, the rains do not come, the children are sometimes unbearable. Where, indeed, is that kingdom of God? And yet, when she bakes bread, the leaven is also hidden and nonetheless permeating the whole dough. Thus the parable of Jesus has a further and different truth to evoke in its hearer. At another moment, in a different time and situation, the parables of Jesus may bring a new and different message to the hearer. We shall deal with that fact in the next chapter, as we examine the parable of the lost sheep and that of the sower. The fourth experience of the woman in Galilee is the fact that the parable is not yet at its end—it continues to speak anew.

Fifth, the short parable ends: "... till it was all leavened." This makes clear that the parable is not a description of an object, but a story about a process. Definitions fix their objects, as if they could not change any more. Stories report various and perhaps very different happenings, sometimes without a detectable continuity, sometimes so that a process becomes visible, but always so that the hearer may expect something more to happen. In the strict sense of the word, Jesus does not teach God, he narrates God. He knows that God is not, again in the strictest sense of the word, teachable. God is, however, reportable. And this is extremely important for the understanding of Jesus and of the God whom he wants to bring into our lives. The woman goes home not having received a new doctrine to possess up to her death, but rather, having been brought into an ongoing story which is directed towards a final goal, "till all will be leavened."

4. *Metaphors, Not Similes*

What then are the parables of Jesus? When I was a student at the University of Marburg we learned to distinguish between parables and allegories. A parable contains one point of comparison, usually illustrating the relation between two persons or things to one another: as the leaven leavens the whole heap of flour, so the kingdom of God permeates the whole of Israel (or even of the world). This is certainly not wrong and it is logical. There are many small things that develop to something much bigger, and that appeals to our common sense. But is it enough? Even in our very short story there are more similarities; the large quantity of flour and the fact that the leaven is hidden in the dough are, in the story of Jesus, probably more than casual embellishments. For when we look at the parable of the prodigal son, it is quite clear that the story runs parallel in many ways to what the people that listen to the story have already experienced and might, under the influence of the story, still experience, when the kingdom of God starts to live with and in them.

In an allegory, every item in the story corresponds to a parallel item in its message. Take, for instance, the dream of king Nebuchadnezzar in Dan 2:31-45. He saw a mighty image with a head of gold, breast and arms of silver, belly and thighs of bronze, legs of iron, and feet partly of iron, partly of clay. Then a stone smote this image so that the whole image was broken into pieces. But nobody could understand that dream until God revealed its meaning to Daniel. The head represented the king's present empire. Breast, belly and legs described three successive kingdoms inferior to Nebuchadnezzar's own kingdom. The feet illustrated a divided kingdom, partly strong and partly brittle. The final stone, which smote the whole image, is the kingdom of God that brings an end to all these worldly kingdoms. Allegories consist of insider language, hiding the truth to outsiders. Only those who have got the key to the secret can understand the message. In an allegory all the images are masks hiding the intended truth behind them. There is no doubt that this is not what Jesus wanted to convey to his hearers in his parables. Therefore we learnt at the universities in the thirties of this century that wherever we find allegorical traits in the tradition of the parables of Jesus, we could be sure that they did not originate from his own preaching. A good example would be Luke 19:12 telling of "the nobleman who went into a far country to receive a kingdom and then return." The hidden truth behind this sentence is, of course, the exaltation of Jesus to God, who will give him his kingdom (Luke 22:29) and his return in the parousia (Acts 1:11 etc.). Again, this is certainly not wrong, but it is not enough.

If the parables of Jesus are not mere illustrations making use of similes, obvious to anybody with common sense, nor allegories open only to insiders, what are they? My successor in Zürich, Hans Weder,[50] rightly understood that the "bricks" of which the parables of Jesus are built are not similes, but metaphors, and that there is more than one point of comparison in them. First let me try to say something about *metaphors*. The classical example of a metaphor in the schoolbooks of rhetoric is the statement: "Achilles (the hero of the Greeks in the war against Troy) is a lion." This is obviously not a simile, because it *identifies* Achilles as a lion though everybody knows that he was a man, not an animal. But in at least one respect "lion" is an excellent term to describe him, not in his unchangeable quality, but in his action. He fights as bravely, as wildly, as victoriously as a lion does within the kingdom of the animals. The metaphor makes sense within a context that tells a story in which his way of fighting is important. In some way, he is not merely to be compared with a lion, in him the pugnacity of the lion is incarnated and becomes a reality.

Or let us consider a modern metaphor. Political speakers, newspapers and television presentations spoke of Mrs. Thatcher as "the iron lady." Again, everybody knows that she does not consist of iron, yet this phrase is one of the best characterizations of her. It is much more graphic

than speaking of a "persevering" or "steadfast" or "unyield-
ing" or "resolute lady." Why? First, it does not appeal for a
logical comparison to be made, by which we might deduce
some similarities. Rather, it appeals to our experiences. Perhaps we once came to iron bars and this was the end of our
journey. Perhaps we once touched iron in winter when the
temperature was below the freezing point and parts of the
skin of our fingers were lost. Or we saw in the museum the
iron armor of a medieval knight and tried to imagine where
his weak points might have been in a battle. Thus real metaphors are only possible within a story in which action
takes place. Second, all the adjectives we mentioned limit a
person much more than the metaphors. The metaphor
"iron" leaves open the ways in which we might specify its
meaning. It has some "band-width," within which we may
understand it. It is not a definition which definitively fixes
the object described by the metaphor in a positive or negative way. Nevertheless, the metaphor is by no means vague.
It creates even a much more precise image within us than
some descriptions using adjectives, because we actually
feel how she is, or better: how she lives and acts. And as in
ordinary life, exactly the same character may be in his or
her acts positive in one situation and negative in another.
The good metaphor does not judge for ever, as if this character were always good or always bad.

Therefore, in a metaphor there is not only that one
point of comparison, which can be illustrated by a simile
and readily apprehended by common sense. In the parables
of Jesus various parts of the story run through the whole
story parallel to various parts of the life of the kingdom of
God. The story evokes various experiences that may become similar experiences of the kingdom of God alive in
our own lives. It is impossible to separate the *bildhälfte*
(the story of Jesus) from the *sachhälfte* (the story that
comes to life in us by the power of the parables of Jesus).
What happens in the story, happens, if it is a good parable,
in the very life of the kingdom in us, or better: in our world.

There is another conclusion to be drawn. Since the message of the parables of Jesus depends on the fact that it is he who tells them, this has to be said explicitly after Easter. During the earthly ministry it was a fact clearly visible to all of his hearers; after Easter the situation changed. Certainly the gospels say that Jesus told those parables. Yet readers in some far away country perhaps knew very little of this Jesus and could not "feel" what this meant. Therefore the church had to emphasize that the parables were still meaningful because they became true in the life and—as is necessary to add after Easter—in the death and the resurrection of Jesus, and will become true in his return at the end of the times. Hence Luke 19:12 is an addition by the post-Easter church, but it is a logical and necessary addition. Implicit christology had to be proclaimed explicitly. We shall deal in the next chapter with two examples of a process in the tradition of the parables and with one more in the tradition of other sayings of Jesus. Yet behind this development in the post-Easter preaching lies the deeper problem of a language that speaks of the transcendent dimension of God's kingdom that becomes living in our earthly lives, shaping them and changing them. We shall see in the fifth chapter that we cannot dispense with a language that also uses "mythological" imagery.[51]

5. *Jesus, the Parable of God.*

We may conclude by stating that, in some way, Jesus himself is *the* parable of God. We shall look at that thesis in the light of our short parable in Luke 13:21.

First, he is the only one who can tell these parables. He claims that in him the kingdom of God—and this is to say: God as the *living* God—comes to the hearers of his parables. "The kingdom of God is like...." If this were not true, everything would be void; it would not be worthwhile to tell the parable or to listen to it. It is only the authority of

Jesus that vouches for the truth of it. We cannot resort to our common senses that show us that it must be so. That, for instance, my debts of sixty million day's wages are simply cancelled, or that God will become like the father of the prodigal son and of the elder brother. When in the parables of Jesus the kingdom of God (the *active* rule of God) approaches the hearers, because the parables become true in Jesus' life, death and resurrection, then he himself is the parable of God, in which God becomes alive among us.

Second, "...like leaven which a woman took." If we want to understand Jesus, we cannot watch him from a distance with a mental reservation that we shall decide later whether to accept him or not. He comes directly into our world and opens himself only to those who dare to get engaged in an encounter with him that might change their lives. It does not necessarily mean a yes or no to a specific doctrine. What this encounter will bring is open to him through whom the kingdom of God starts to live in us and our world. But just as a parable cannot be understood if we do not let ourselves be dragged into it, and even as love among human beings never becomes true if we only want to look at it from the outside, so Jesus and his stories come to life as *the* parable of God only when we start to live and to listen from *inside* them.

Third, "three measures of flour...": Jesus is *the* parable of God, because all the amazing traits which appear in the center of his stories, become true in his ministry. In him the kingdom of God manifests itself in such an unexpected, surprising way. "If it is by the finger of God that I cast out demons, then the kingdom of God has come upon you" (Luke 11:20, Q). And if the one who has just died with a loud cry has truly been the son of God, as even a gentile confesses, then this kingdom comes to life also for those who are totally crushed, helpless and hopeless.

Fourth, "... and hid it under..." : Jesus is *the* parable of God, not only because the amazing traits of the stories of Jesus that are glorious and welcome manifestations of God's grace and love and of his final victory became true in his life, but also because of the hiddenness of that grace and love and victory. Where could it be better hidden than in the weakness of this Jesus, rejected more and more and finally disposed of on the cross? And the mystery of the power of God in and through this weakness, the resurrection of the crucified one, the "folly of the word of the cross" that becomes the "power of God," is to be found in Jesus, because he who has been raised and preached to the world became "our wisdom, our righteousness and sanctification and redemption" (1 Cor 1:18,30).[52] Therefore all his parables will live on and speak again and again in different ways and into different situations. Basically, it will always be the same word, but we cannot limit the way in which this message will meet us today and tomorrow. Jesus remains "the living one."

Fifth, "...till it was all leavened." Jesus is *the* parable of God, because he is the guarantor for the kingdom of God, which became present in his ministry and will be fulfilled finally. Without him, there is no hope. But all his ministry, all his words and all his deeds, his dying and his rising were always open towards the future of God who will vindicate him and his words and deeds. Jesus is the living "principle of hope" for and in our world.

All this is, of course, the language of faith. I'll try to show at the end of Chapter Three (pp. 51-52) that, in my view, this is the only possible answer if we do not want to declare Jesus mad or burdened with some kind of religious mania.

III

JESUS THE PREACHER AND HEALER, THE FRIEND OF TAX COLLECTORS AND SINNERS

In the preceding chapter I tried to show how the person and authorship of Jesus is central for the understanding of his parables. He tells of surprising, unexpected happenings, because things that nobody would have expected become true in him. By acting and speaking in this way he claims that the kingdom of God is becoming a present reality in his very ministry. The fact that he tells parables in such a way thus implies a christology. In the first half of this chapter we shall see how this implicit christology becomes explicit in the tradition of two parables (the lost sheep and the sower) and of a group of other sayings of Jesus (the sermon on the mount). This is a *dogmatic* process. It leads to the confession of the post-Easter church that Jesus is the messiah who brings sinners back to God (Luke 15:1-2) and brings about the harvest of God (Mark 4:20). That is to say that Jesus is the Christ (Matt 11:2,5-6). But it is also an *ethical* process. This christology, as it is adapted to post-Easter situations, becomes also a challenge to the church. It warns against all self-sufficiency with a Christian ideology and points to dangers threatening the group of believers (Matt 18:12-14; Mark 4:14-19; Matt 7:13-27). In the second half of the chapter we shall ask how far such an implicit christology is to be detected in the deeds of Jesus (healings, table-fellowship) and in what he said directly and indirectly about his own person and ministry (including the term "the son of man").

1. *The parable of the lost sheep: Luke 15:3-7*

Jesus tells of the shepherd who left ninety-nine sheep in the wilderness and went and found the one sheep that had gone astray. What is surprising in this parable? First, when David left his flock to fight against the giant Goliath, he got a keeper for the sheep (1 Sam 17:20). Nothing is said about a keeper here.[53] Thus the extreme value of this one sheep is emphasized, since the shepherd takes the risk of losing his other ninety-nine sheep. In the parallel parable of the woman who lost her silver coin, this particular emphasis is lacking. But just as the shepherd calls all his friends to celebrate in both versions of the parable of the lost sheep (Luke 15:5-7; Matt 18:13), so also does she (Luke 15:9-10), and the schoolboy who made the comment that this was a silly woman because she would have spent on coffee and biscuits more than she had found, was quite right! In both versions of the lost sheep parable as well as in that of the lost coin, overflowing joy is stressed very much. This is the central point of the three passages, and equally underlined in all three. When Jesus told these stories he urged his hearers to rejoice, because they should identify themselves with that sheep or that coin which went astray and was found.

The summary in Luke 15:7—"There will be more joy in heaven over one sinner who repents than over ninety-nine righteous persons who need no repentance" (and similarly in v.10)—seems to be a secondary interpretation, since neither the sheep nor the coin returned to its owner. Rather, it was the owner who went out to seek and find them. Thus the two parables actually tell what happened in the very act of Jesus' telling the parables. The listeners understood and shared this immense joy as they were "found" by the shepherd or the woman, and were brought home to their God. Thus, in this implicit christology, the figures of shepherd and woman are metaphors for Jesus in whose ministry this seeking and finding comes to its goal. Already, in the secondary summary (Luke 15:7) just referred to, it is made explicit that it is the salvation of the sinner that is proclaimed in these stories and thus also the act of repentance is included. When Luke and Matthew inserted this parable of the sheep into their gospels, they did so in the context of their respective situations and underlined what Jesus meant for their particular problems.

Luke introduces this parable: "The tax collectors and sinners were all drawing near to hear Jesus. And the Pharisees and scribes murmured saying: 'This man receives sinners and eats with them.' " Luke seems to know of people who do not accept a Jesus who brings low and morally doubtful persons back to the people of God. Thus Luke says explicitly that Jesus is that shepherd who found the sinners so that all the angels in heaven would rejoice, and Luke warns against any rejection of the one by whom the kingdom of God comes to all of us. Implicit christology becomes explicit.

Matthew lives in a community that needs some church order to guide them in how to behave towards their brothers and sisters who might need help. The congregation seems to be a bit complacent. Are they not the people of God, the flock of sheep found by their savior Jesus? And they may sing in a very self-satisfied way: "His sheep are we...." Thus the parable of Jesus leads more and more to self-satisfaction. Therefore Matthew forms a whole chapter of church orders and into this chapter he inserts the parable of the lost sheep (18:12-14). It is then followed by the advice to pray for fellow-members, to speak to them, to forgive them seventy times seven, and it is introduced with the warning "never to despise these little ones." Again, the parable speaks in a new language and conveys a new truth. It may say: "Was there not a woman in your church three weeks ago? She was not there two weeks ago nor last Sunday and you did not even think of going to her and seeing how she is." And again, Jesus becomes the living lord who still moves his disciples to follow him, this time with an emphasis on the ethical consequences. Implicit christology becomes explicit as the admonition of the living and exalted Lord.

2. *The parable of the sower: Mark 4:3-9*

What is surprising in this parable? First, the harvest is almost miraculously rich. A yield of one hundred-fold is just possible—for instance when two ears grow out of the grain— but very unusual. *Jesus* tells us so and *he* urges us to get ears to hear it. Now in his preaching this harvest is already growing. Whereas the failures of the sower are all reported in the Greek aorist tense, which emphasizes a definite final event, the verbs of the last sentence (except "fell") are put in the imperfect tense which describes a long process which goes on and on. This final harvest is narrated briefly in contrast to the failures that are described at some surprising length, since it is not the story of a grumbling peasant, but of one who wants to praise the final harvest. Again, the ministry of Jesus becomes visible behind the story. It seems to lead from failure to failure as his message is rejected. Nothing is visible of the kingdom of God that he announces. One sees only birds and rocks and thorns, which all destroy the seed. Yet this seed lives and grows and will bring the victory of God's kingdom, though it is still often invisible to human eyes. "Let anyone with ears to hear listen."

When the church read this parable some thirty years later, it knew that *Jesus* was the sower and it saw that the seed was already "yielding a hundredfold." "The sower sows the word" in v.14 is actually explicit christology and it might also be understood to include all those who, committed and authorized by him, proclaimed his message, the "word" or the "kerygma," all over the world. Yet this explicit christology, correct as it is, also became dangerous. We might imagine the church then thinking: "Were there not, some decades ago, only twelve disciples and now there are around 1200 in this one town? The crows and the rocks and the thorns have disappeared, and so too the Pharisees, who tried to destroy the seed planted by Jesus, the 'hard-boiled' unbelievers, and the Romans who killed Jesus and even some of his followers." Thus, the parable merely buttressed their complacency. It had to be read in a new way, lest it worked contrarily to the way in which Jesus intended it to. Thus the interpretation following in 4:14-20 contains many terms that we never find in the sayings of Jesus, but often in the apostolic letters. I think it has been added by the post-Easter church to convey the reinterpretation that birds and rocks and thorns are primarily not outside, but *inside* the church. Here again, the Greek tenses differ. Speaking of those who fail, the verbs emphasize that God (or the risen Lord) goes on sowing for a long time, whereas the hearers hear and turn away definitively. Speaking of those that hear the word and bear fruit, it is exactly the other way around: the sower throws his seed just once and for all into them (the good soil) and they continue listening to him on and on. Again, implicit christology becomes—and emphatically so—the admonition of the living and exalted Lord.

Let me add as a kind of footnote a few words on the very difficult text between the parable and the interpretation: "To you has been given the secret of the kingdom of God, but for those outside everything is in parables, so that they may indeed see but not perceive and may indeed hear but not understand; lest they should turn again and be forgiven." In v.33 Mark says explicitly that Jesus spoke in parables to the people, "as they were able to hear the word" and that "to his own disciples he explained everything." How can we reconcile these two statements? The first one in vv.10-12 leads directly to v.13, where Jesus says to the twelve (that is: to those "inside"): "Do you not understand

this parable? How then will you understand all the parables?" In fact, even the twelve are "outsiders," not understanding what Jesus wanted to say. In 8:17-18 Jesus even
asks the twelve: "Do you not yet perceive or understand?
Are your hearts hardened? Having eyes do you not see?
And having ears do you not hear?" Mark emphasizes the
suffering and dying of Jesus so much that it shapes the
structure of his whole gospel.[54] In the first half of his Gali-
lean ministry the three sections of the gospel begin with the
call of the first disciples (1:14-20), the selection of the
twelve (3:13-19) and the sending of them (6:7-13), and
each time they end with the rejection of Jesus—by the
Pharisees and Herodians planning his death (3:1-6), by Jesus' fellow-citizens (6:1-6) and by the disciples themselves,
whose "hearts are hardened," who "having eyes do not see,
and having ears do not hear" (8:14-21, cf. 4:11-12!). The
second half of Jesus' ministry in Galilee is structured by
three predictions of the suffering of the son of man, always
followed by a total misunderstanding on the part of the disciples (8:31-33; 9:31-34; 10:33-37). Then follows the story
of Jesus' passion in Jerusalem. In the history of the post-
Easter church Mark has learnt in a radical way what the
grace of God means: *all* our hearts are hardened, *all* our
eyes are blind and *all* our ears are stopped up, as long as he,
Jesus, does not open them. "None is righteous, no, not
one," writes Paul, referring to Eccles 7:20 and Ps 53. But
Jesus does open hearts, eyes and ears still, as he did for his
disciples and through them now to all who read their writings—including the gospel of Mark.

3. *The sermon on the mount: Matt 5-7*

Something similar is to be seen in the sermon on the
mount. There is a wide consensus about the authenticity of
the sayings in Matt 5:21-22 and 27-28: "You have heard
that it was said to the men of old: You shall not kill but I
say to you that everyone who is angry with his brother shall
be liable to judgment," and: "You have heard that it was

said: You shall not commit adultery. But I say to you that everyone who looks at a woman lustfully has already committed adultery." With the exception of Jesus' rejection of a certificate of divorce in contrast to Deut 24:1-4 (in Matt 5:31-32) these antitheses do not annul the law, but rather interpret the law in a rigorous way. They actually teach that the law of God is not like the law of the police, in which the speed limit of fifty-five miles an hour allows—and even invites me—to drive almost at, but not over, that limit. Obviously the law of God does not invite me to kill my brother halfway and to commit only a little bit of adultery so long as I do not quite go to the end! Moreover, Jesus does not introduce his words like a rabbi: "It is written and this means...," not even like the prophets: "Thus says the lord." He puts his own: "...but I say to you" over against the word of God in the scriptures. If neither the wording of the scriptures nor the inspired word of the prophets is the decisive authority, what is then? In an unheard of way Jesus rejects obedience to the letter of the law and the prophets in favor of obedience to the will of God *behind* the law, but manifest now in Jesus' own interpretation. The law of God is not a code that one can fulfill literally; it is rather like a sign post which shows me that even the first step in the wrong direction is a wrong step. But in this case, nobody except God alone is able to judge whether or not we are fulfilling the will of God behind the law. Jesus gives us extreme liberty and at the same time extreme responsibility in this matter.

The tax-collector who has not kept to the letter of the law is justified, not the Pharisee who did (Luke 18:14). Jesus himself is keeping the sabbath holy (Exod 20:8) by healing the sick—against the letter of the law—and not those who obey the law which forbids any work on this day (Mark 2:27-28).

Again there is an implicit christology behind this and many of the other words of Jesus in this sermon.

Again, this becomes explicit later. Since many sayings in Matt 5-7 are to be found in various parts of Mark and Luke, it was very probably Matthew who collected what were originally independent sayings of Jesus together to make his sermon on the mount, exactly as he did with the deeds of Jesus in the following chapters 8-9. In his chapter 11, Matthew starts with the Baptist who heard in prison of "the deeds of the Christ" (only Matthew formulates it in this way) and who then sent two disciples to ask Jesus: "Are you he who is to come...?" (which is to say "the Christ"?) Jesus answers this problem of christology by saying: "Go and tell John what you hear and see: the blind receive their sight and the lame walk, lepers are cleansed and the deaf hear and the dead are raised up and the poor have the good news preached to them. And blessed is he who takes no offence at me." This is exactly what Jesus reported in chapters 5-9. They could hear the sermon on the mount, which begins: "Blessed are the poor" and they could see the deeds of Jesus in all the details mentioned there.[55] The sermon on the mount and the stories of the healings have a christological function. They show that Jesus is the Christ indeed and invite the reader to believe in him. The intervening chapter 10 even promises that the preaching and healings of Jesus will go on in his church so that people will see something of the authority of Jesus also among his followers.[56]

Even the Matthean structure of the sermon on the mount expresses the view that Jesus is the messianic teacher of the law. The beatitudes in 5:3-10 correspond to the final parable, which shows that the value of the house we build lies in its foundation on the rock, not in its beauty, its turrets and terraces and swimming pools (7:24-27). The installation of the disciples as prophets of this time (5:11-16) corresponds to the warning against the false prophets in 7:13-23. Both pairs of passages frame the two decisive words which include the core of the sermon: on the one hand 5:17—"Think not that I have come to abolish the law and the prophets," and on the other 7:12—"Whatever you wish that men would do to you, do so to them; for this is the law and the prophets." In Matthew's understanding Jesus states that the law should lead us in all our activities, but in a way that the commandment to love God and our neighbor is always superior,[57] exactly as communal laws have to yield to the superior constitution of the state. As long as only our own welfare is at stake, we should, for instance, keep the law of the sabbath strictly— even if it could cost our life (cf. Matt 24:20, where "or on a sabbath" is added to the same saying in Mark 13:18); but when the food rules hinder the gentiles from joining the people of God, the commandment to love makes these rules obsolete: "Not what goes into the mouth defiles a man, but what comes out of the mouth" (15:11). It is an enormous liberty and responsibility that Jesus has given to his church, and also to the church (in Syria?) at the time of Matthew. In chapters 5-11 Matthew shows, on the one hand, his concern for a *dogmatic* christology, for a faith that sees in Jesus "the Christ," evidenced by his words and deeds. On the other hand, we see his equal concern for an *ethical* christology, which emphasizes that the work and the authority of Jesus Christ should live on in his church, so much so that love for one's neighbor becomes stronger than even the wish to save one's own life.

4. *Jesus the healer*

Jesus healed people. We can not be sure how many, but he certainly performed healings. There is direct evidence in the letters of Paul that healing continued in the early church.[58] Yet healings were not expected of the messiah; so only prophets like Elijah and Elisha could be seen as providing prototypes. Whether the Hellenistic world of that time knew itinerant charismatic healers is uncertain. Collections of such stories postdate the gospels.[59] Besides, there is a striking difference between the Hellenistic collections of the second century and the gospel stories. Faith is mentioned in the Hellenistic stories too, but only at the end;

the miracle should lead the reader to believe in the god who performed it. In the gospels, the place of faith is at the beginning of the story; Jesus asks for faith or states that there is faith, which will heal or has healed the sick person. Thus the relation of the sick person to God is prior to—and the basis of—healing.[60] However it is not the cause of healing in the strictest sense of the term. Jesus himself evokes such trust in God by his very presence or by his words. He may even, as in the story of the paralytic in Mark 2:5, see the faith not of the sick person, but of those that brought him to Jesus. Faith is not an achievement to be fulfilled in advance; it too is the gift of God. But it shows that the restitution of the relationship with God is the decisive event, which then expresses itself in bodily healing.

We know that miracles cannot prove God. There was an Indian in Zürich some decades ago who had a dagger driven through his heart, a feat he had demonstrated before in other places. My colleagues in the medical faculty controlled and x-rayed everything. There was not the slightest doubt that a miracle had happened; he should have been dead, but he did not follow suit and remained alive. The experiment was even repeated afterwards. Yet we did not believe in that man and he did not want to lead us to believe in his god. We also know that miracle stories are often enlarged in the course of the tradition, so that we cannot be absolutely sure what originally happened. However, it is not so important to know exactly how many and what kind of miracles Jesus really performed. On the one hand, there is no doubt that he did heal and on the other hand, according to Jesus himself, his healing was but an expression of something which went deeper than bodily health. We cannot be sure that all the references to faith are authentic reports of the exact words of Jesus, but the emphasis on faith (which has no real parallels in Jewish or Hellenistic literature) and not on the miraculous divine power of the healer seems to be his emphasis indeed. This claim to bring God's presence into the lives of sick people, to reunite them again with their Lord in faith, is a kind of implicit christology. Again it is made explicit later. Of the people in Nazareth Mark writes: "And Jesus could do no mighty work there . . . and he marvelled because of their unbelief" (6:6).

This faith was not merely an individual personal experience for the one who was sick and was healed. In Luke 11:20 (cf. Matt 12:28) Jesus says: "If it is by the finger of God that I cast out demons, then the kingdom of God has come upon you." This is a statement without parallels either in Judaism or in the early church and therefore, has a high probability of being an authentic saying of Jesus.[61] Wherever Jesus is healing, the finger of God is moving. The very person of God comes in an act of love to people. We may not yet see God fully, but we can experience God, we can feel God's finger touching us. This means that the kingdom of God is, according to Jesus, already present in his work.[62] In his healings it reaches out to those people who allow themselves to be touched by it.

A similar statement is to be found in Luke 17:20-21. When the Pharisees asked Jesus when the kingdom of God was coming, he answered them: "The kingdom of God is not coming with signs to be observed; nor will they say 'Lo, here it is!' or 'There!' for behold the kingdom of God is in the midst of you." Whether Jesus wanted to say: "in my own preaching and healing it is present"—or: "it is up to you whether it is present or not," is still debated.[63] Whatever the right interpretation may be, again the message of Jesus is unparalleled by Jewish or early Christian assertions. And again, it is not a simple statement of fact that one could just observe and accept. Rather it is an appeal to see what Jesus can see, to trust him so that one receives Jesus' eyes to see God as he sees him. In these two passages implicit christology is clearly visible.

Yet we would misunderstand them if we did not, at the same time, realize that the healings of Jesus never were visible signs of a triumphant messiah, in whose acts the victorious power of God has become visible to all. There is another saying of Jesus about the presence of the kingdom (which is authentic without any doubt according to E. Käsemann[64]), in Matt 11:12—"From the days of John the Baptist until now the kingdom of heaven has suffered violence and men of violence take it by force." No doubt the kingdom of God is present; the question is, in what way? The violence against it is visible. And if Jesus was not extremely naïve, he must have reckoned with the possibility of death as he ascended to Jerusalem.[65] It is in Jesus' life and death that the kingdom of God manifested itself in both ways, in visible help to poor and sick people and in the rejection of the one in whom this help became a reality. Whether people can encounter this kingdom of God depends on their ability to see it not only in its more beneficial manifestations, but also in the contrary experiences of life—and especially in the passion story, which we will turn to in Chapter IV.

Two more healing stories are characteristic of the ministry of Jesus. When Jesus healed the ten lepers and one of them came back to praise God, Jesus said according to Luke 17:11-19: "Were not ten cleansed? Where are the nine?" and then to the one who returned: "Rise and go your way, your faith has made you well" (or: "has saved you"). The decisive question is whether these healings become transparent for a salvation which goes far beyond physical healing. And it is Jesus again who brings this salvation and declares that the healed leper is saved. In an even more impressive way, Jesus says to the woman who has not been healed physically at all (in the story of Luke 7:36-50): "Your faith has saved (or healed) you, go in peace," then explains that to the reproachful Pharisee: "Her sins, which are many, are forgiven, for she loved much." There is another story that speaks of forgiveness of sins. When the paralytic was brought to Jesus, he told him: "My son, your sins are forgiven," and later on he healed him (Mark 2:1-12). The authenticity of both pericopes is questionable. Luke

17:11-19 does not appear in other sources, and Mark 2:1-12 might be a compilation of two different stories, one about forgiveness of sins and the discussion of Jesus with his opponents, the other about the healing of this man. Therefore we can say with certainty no more than this is the way in which the followers of Jesus understood (possibly after Easter only) the importance of the "faith" motif in the healings of Jesus. "Magic and meal," healing and table-fellowship are, in Crossan's view,[66] the two poles around which the Jesus-movement turned. Let us, therefore, turn to the second of these two poles.

5. Jesus, friend of tax collectors and sinners

Table fellowship was certainly a very important feature of the ministry of Jesus. In contrast to all other religious communities of their time, the early Christians had no temple, no statues, no priests, no special cult; the only thing visible was a table with a meal around which they came together every week. It was the continuation of the table fellowship of Jesus, and especially of that meal on the last evening together. It was a definitive gift from God and a central manifestation of the truth the church brought to the world. Table fellowship was already important in the time of the earthly ministry of Jesus, as is proven by the various accusations against him: "Behold a glutton and a drunkard, a friend of tax collectors and sinners" (Luke 7:34, Q). The Pharisees and the scribes murmured: "This man receives sinners and eats with them" (Luke 15:2). They said: "Why does he eat with tax collectors and sinners?" (Mark 2:16, also pOxy 1224, p. 175). In Jericho all murmured: "He has gone to be the guest of a man who is a sinner" (Luke 19:7). Q and Mark and the special tradition of Luke agree on the fact that the table-fellowship Jesus shared upset many people. Obviously everybody understood that they represented much more than a simple comradeship of Tom, Dick and Harry— that it was more than just openness and egalitarianism.[67] In the time of Jesus, the people with whom he ate and drank were regarded as "sinners," outsiders, and even ostracized people because they were seen as having relinquished God and spurned his commandments. Whether Jesus ever spoke the words "Your sins are forgiven" (probably, he did so) or not, these people found in the encounter with Jesus their way back into communion with God and into the membership of the people of God. Forgiveness of sins happened, often, maybe always, without any outspoken confession and absolution. The fact that Jesus acted as if he stood in place of God, was an implicit christological statement. The scribes (maybe in a later interpretation of the tradition) made it more explicit: "Who can forgive sins but God alone?" (Mark 2:7).

6. *The status of Jesus manifested in his acts and words*

The fact that Jesus called disciples to follow him is unparalleled both in Judaism and in the early church, and is testified to in all four gospels.[68] In contrast to the rabbis, Jesus did not wait for people to ask him whether he would allow them to follow him; on the contrary, it seemed that he sent home such applicants (Mark 5:19). A student of a rabbi hoped to become a rabbi as great or even greater than his teacher. Jesus never nurtured such hopes of becoming a greater "son of man" or whatever the title might be. Following him would never mean greatness and glory, but rather suffering and death and his disciples had to leave all that would hinder them from following him. It is difficult to imagine that all the radical warnings of Jesus could be of a late origin. Life and death for all eternity might depend on the "yes" and "no" given to his call to follow.[69] In a wider sense this is true for all his hearers: "It will be more tolerable on that day (of judgment) for Sodom" than for those who fail to hear his call. "Woe to you Chorazin, woe to you Bethsaida, it shall be more tolerable for Tyre and Sidon than for you!" (Luke 10:12-14, Q). For, "here is more than Solomon, more than Jonah" (Luke 11:31-32, Q), and "here is something greater than the temple" (Matt 12:6). It is not easy to imagine that warnings to such small and unimportant towns could have been created later, and especially statements not about *the one* who is greater, Jesus, but about some*thing* greater. Of himself Jesus says: "Who is greater, one who sits at table or one who serves?... But I am among you as one who serves" (Luke 22:27, which might well be an authentic word of Jesus).[70] Finally, Jesus has called God "abba" (father), which is a term of intimate love used by children or adults. Admittedly, this is reported only in Mark 14:36 and some argue that this might be a retro-projection from the liturgy of the church, which still kept the Aramaic term (Rom 8:15, Gal 4:6). This is not impossible, though not probable. At the least, Jesus used the term "father" in his prayers, so that he seems to have always spoken either of "my father" or "your father" ("our father" only when Jesus teaches his disciples how *they* should pray), though the evidence has a slender basis. As an address to God, "abba" is unique and "father" (without any other title) rare in Jewish prayers. Though we cannot be totally sure, it seems at least that this usage was typical of Jesus.[71]

Yet Jesus never calls himself messiah (cf. note 73) or son of God (at the most indirectly: Mark 12:35-37) or servant of God, if the testimony of the synoptic authors is correct. We do find "the son" used over against "the father" (Mark 13:32; Luke 10:22 Q) which implies sonship, but it emphasizes rather subordination under God, not the superior status of Jesus over all people. We do find the confession of Peter to Jesus as the messiah—which Jesus does not deny—but according to Mark 8:29-31 he merely "charged them to tell no one about him" and spoke at once of "the son of man," who has to suffer and be killed. Jesus repeats this change to "the son of man," when the high-priest asks him in the trial hearing whether he considers himself to be the messiah, and Jesus affirms it in a direct *or* indirect way (cf. the differing traditions in Mark 14:62/Matt 26:64, and

Luke 22:67-68). All these reports may be historical, as I personally think they are, but they are not definitely so, and anyway the situation and the context limit their assessment as unambiguous selfdesignations of Jesus.

Therefore we are left with the phrase "the son of man." It is to be found exclusively on the lips of Jesus (about 80 times, if the Synoptic parallels are all counted) and only once differently (Stephen, in Acts 7:56). Moreover, it appears always with two articles "*the* son of *the* man," which is different from its use in Jewish writings,[72] with the exception of the Similitudes in Ethiopic Enoch, the date of which is still not certain. On the other hand, Jesus is called "Christ" (messiah) over 500 times in the New Testament, but according to all four gospels Jesus uses the word (almost) never.[73] One result of an extensive debate which has continued over many years seems to be clear: Jesus did speak of "the son of man," very probably also calling himself "the son of man." The term was not a well defined title. For decades most scholars thought that the expectation of the parousia of this "son of man" was the core and the origin of this self-designation. I myself suggested already in 1959 that the sayings of the present "son of man" might be the oldest ones,[74] and this seems to be accepted more and more today.[75] *Casey, Hare* and *Crossan* suggest that Jesus used the phrase "the son of man" as we use "one." We may say: "One has to be cautious" meaning: "I have to be cautious." But if Jesus had *only* spoken in such a discreet and humble way like people who don't dare to say "I," would that have been so impressive that his disciples developed the phrase further to be a very specific and central term that is used emphatically—and then only by Jesus himself? I still think that Jesus used it, as a kind of "implicit christology," just because it was *ambiguous,* being both a modest circumlocution for "I" and a not yet fixed, veiled hint of divine authority. The background for the latter usage is, of course, Daniel 7, where the son of man flies on the clouds of heaven—according to the interpretation, by the way, *to*

God, and not *from* God to the earth. This would fit well with the way Jesus claimed to speak and to act with the highest possible authority, but not in a doctrinal form, using titles that people could simply take over and repeat, like "Christ" or "son of God" or "servant of God." Rather, he used a phrase that challenged his hearers so that they were puzzled and wondered whether he spoke of himself or of another one,[76] whether he was merely humble or rather making a claim for heavenly authority.

So Jesus never gives a final definition of himself. People have to listen to him and to see his whole life and death and then find their own answer, using the words with which they can express the truth that has come into their lives, challenging, changing and saving them.[77] Let me illustrate what I mean by a trivial example. Suppose I am going to a party and meet there a nice young man. He has had bad experiences with pastors. If I tell him that I am a pastor, he has a fixed pattern of what a pastor is and I have to fight against that picture the whole evening. Perhaps I may ultimately convince him that I am not what he thought a pastor to be; nevertheless the whole evening's discussion is constrained by his fixed ideas, until, hopefully I can overcome them. On the other hand, suppose he does not know who I am and we have an excellent discussion, agreeing on vital and decisive points. When he asks me at midnight what profession I am in and I tell him that I am a pastor, he may tell his friend next morning: "Do you know Mr. such and such? *He* is a pastor!"—and "pastor" has for him received a totally new meaning. This is exactly what has happened to the early church. After the crucifixion, the words "Christ," "son of God" and "servant of God" have received a totally new meaning and after Easter the followers of Jesus could tell everybody: "This Jesus really is the Christ, the son of God, the servant of God."[78]

So we can conclude that Jesus may never have declared himself to be the Christ, the son of God or the ser-

vant of God. Yet he taught in parables that would have remained incredible fairy-tales if God himself had not given
him the authority to do so. He healed people and claimed
that in this way the kingdom of God was already reaching
out to all those who were witnessing them. The definitive
forgiveness of sins was granted in his table-fellowship with
sinners and the scribes were quite right when they asked
"Who can forgive sins but God alone?" (Mark 2:7). He
called people to follow him, because nothing on earth was
more important than following him. He declared that in his
preaching and acting the kingdom of God was present in a
way that it had not been present in all the prophets or kings
before him, even in John the Baptist. He spoke to God as
his "abba" in a way no other human being ever thought of
speaking. Who then was he, if not a prophet or king or eschatological messenger of God? *Either* he was an example
of religious mania—*or* the one in whom God came to this
world uniquely and definitively. Thus the historical question becomes a direct and very relevant question for us:
Who is he for me today? We may have difficulties with
some of the traditional terms, we may even be forced to
state these old terms in a different way when speaking to
contemporary humanity and to ourselves as contemporary
people! We may not even be able to find the right formulas
and terms, but if we don't wish to lose our very lives—our
sense of meaning and purpose—we should let him, the living Jesus Christ, enter our lives, speak to us, act in us,
guide us, until (and this sentence in 1 John 3:2 has become
perhaps the most important one for me in the last ten years)
"we shall see him, as he is."

IV

JESUS THE CRUCIFIED

In all four gospels—and even more so in most New Testament letters (especially in those of Paul and his school)—the death and resurrection of Jesus are more central than his words and deeds. This, of course, mirrors the emphasis of the church after Good Friday and Easter. We therefore have to investigate first what we know about the facts on which all these statements are founded. Second, we should very carefully ask how far there might be an implicit christology in the way Jesus looked ahead to his death and resurrection. Third, we may point to some trends in the interpretation of these events by the earliest church.

1. *The Crucifixion of Jesus: the facts.*

That Jesus was crucified, with some cooperation between the Jews and gentile Romans, is not to be doubted.[79] It is almost the only fact about Jesus that is clearly reported also by non-Christian authors. The Roman historian Tacitus tells us around 100 A.D. that the Christians were revolting against the emperor Nero in the middle of the first century and that they were named after one called Christ, who had been crucified in the reign of Tiberius by Pontius Pilate.[80] Later testimonies in Roman literature may depend on this notice. But the book of Josephus, a Jewish historian born in Jerusalem, was written in 93/94 A.D. in Rome, and contains a long passage about Jesus.[81] As it stands in the manuscripts we possess, which have been copied and recopied

by Christians over a long period of time, it says that Jesus
was the messiah, prophesied by the prophets, crucified and
risen. This is a very unexpected confession for a Jew. Josephus was not a Jewish Christian, as all his writings clearly
show. So these sentences must have been added by a Christian copyist. Probably Josephus wrote only of "a wise man
Jesus" (as we find it at the beginning of this passage), who
taught as a Jewish teacher and was crucified by Pilate. But
even if this Christian copyist had written and inserted the
whole passage (including that very vague designation of Jesus as a "wise man"), there is another reference to Jesus in
Josephus. There he reports on the martyrdom of James,
who is described as "the brother of Jesus, the so-called
Christ" (which is certainly not the way a Christian would
write).[82] Brothers of Jesus[83] are also mentioned in all four
canonical gospels, the gospel of Thomas, Acts, and by Paul
in 1 Cor. 9:5 (and here very casually).[84] Thus, even if we
were supercritical, there is no doubt that Jesus lived and
was crucified in the time of Pilate.[85]

2. *Did Jesus ever speak of his coming death?*

But what was this execution of Jesus? A well de-
served punishment for a crime? A deplorable error of jus-
tice? A saving event? If so, in what sense?

Whether Jesus himself gave a clear answer to that
question is difficult to say. If there is any truth in our tradition, Jesus saw his whole ministry as given to him by God.
What happened to him was due to the will of God. Unless
he was completely given over to despair as the end approached, he could not think otherwise of what came to
him in Jerusalem. Anyone with some common sense could
not exclude the possibility of a final rejection and even
death there. Jesus interpreted his whole ministry as a final
call of God back to obedience and as the final offering for
forgiveness of sins, grace and salvation. This took place in
his preaching and all his actions and reactions, so he would

also have included his potential fate in Jerusalem within his trust of the father and as a part of his openness to serve all those whom God would lead to him. In this sense, his death was for him part of his "pro-existence," his *life for* God and for all his fellow humans.[86] But did he ever express such a view in a clear statement?

The open predictions of his death and resurrection have, in my view, been formulated after Easter.[87] Otherwise it would be difficult to understand the shock and despair of Jesus' disciples, who fled in total disorientation after Jesus' arrest so that none of them was left in Jerusalem to carry out the highest duty of a disciple—to care for the burial of Jesus. It was an outsider, Joseph of Arimathea, mentioned in all four gospels, who had to do so and—again differing from Crossan and Lüdemann[88]—I cannot imagine that the later church invented such a person. Whatever the truth about the burial of Jesus by Joseph of Arimathea may be, it is clear that the disciples did not take charge of this burial. "They all forsook him and fled" (Mark 14:50). This does not necessarily mean that they left Jerusalem at once— Peter is there during the night—but at the latest they would have left by the time the execution of Jesus actually took place and returned to their homes in Galilee.[89]

But there are some more general sayings of Jesus, which might be authentic: "I must go on my way today and tomorrow and the day following; for it cannot be that a prophet should perish away from Jerusalem" (Luke 13:33). This could be a word of Jesus, for the church after Easter would not call Jesus a "prophet."[90] Yet it is also possible that Luke created it himself.[91] The next verse ("O Jerusalem, Jerusalem, killing the prophets and stoning those who are sent to you...") stems from Q and seems to be authentic, whether spoken in Jerusalem (as Matt 23:37 locates it) or in the situation of Luke 13:34.[92] The Q-saying in Luke 9:58 (and gospel of Thomas 86) shows how much Jesus was aware of the insecurity of his life: "Foxes have holes and

birds of the air have nests; but the son of man has nowhere
to lay his head." Since the beginning of our century it has
been suggested that "son of man" simply meant "man."
Linguistically this is quite possible and is taken up again by
Crossan.[93] But then the saying would only make sense during wartime or among fugitives, and before the war of 66-
70 A.D. it is difficult to imagine such a general situation in
which this word could have been created.

There are many more sayings of Jesus that expect
trouble, persecution and perhaps even death for himself and
the disciples. In Mark 8:34-37 and its parallels as well as in
Matt 10:38-39/Luke 14:27; 17:33 Q, the reference to "taking up one's cross" could even have been made by Jesus,
because "the sight of criminals on their way to crucifixion
was familiar enough in Roman Palestine."[94] But it might be
that Jesus spoke instead of "bearing his yoke."[95] Be this as
it may, even without this phrase the warnings are clear
enough. Gospel of Thomas 55 and 67 reflect these sayings,
and John, who very rarely refers to any suffering of Jesus,
shows a knowledge of them (12:24-26) and emphasizes the
coming martyrdom of the disciples (16:2, cf. 21:18-19).
That they are like sheep sent among the wolves is predicted
in Luke 10:3/Matt 10:16 Q.[96] Finally, Mark 8:33 ("Get behind me, Satan!") seems to be an authentic word of Jesus[97]
and it is difficult to imagine it occurring in a situation other
than that underlying Mark 8:32, where Peter warns against
going up to Jerusalem.

The interpretation of the "sign of Jonah" as pointing
to death, burial and resurrection of Jesus in Matt 12:40 is
the later reflection of the church. According to Mark 8:11-
12, "no sign will be given to this generation." According to
Luke 11:30 (parallel to Matt 12:40 Q) Jesus said only: "As
Jonah became a sign to the men of Nineveh, so will the son
of man be to this generation," then going on (Luke 11:31-
32 almost in literal conformity with Matt 12:41-42) to the
description of the last judgment, in which the men of Nine-

veh will condemn this generation, because they (the Nine-
vites) repented at the preaching of Jonah. This leads to the
problem of whether Jesus has identified himself with this
"son of man" (cf. pp. 50-51), and whether he also did so in
other eschatological sayings. If so, he has at least reckoned
with his death and his vindication by God. The same is true
for many words in the eschatological discourses (Mark
13:1-37 and its parallels; Luke 17:22-37 and 12:35-53, partly Q) including predictions of persecution for Jesus' followers. This is to be discussed below (pp. 85-88).

To summarize: there seems to be sufficient evidence that Jesus was at least aware of the dangers threatening him. In view of his rejection by more and more people,
he certainly could not exclude the possibility of a "head-on
collision" occurring as he approached Jerusalem and en-
tered the "lion's den." But did he speak definitely of his
death and, more importantly, did he interpret it?

3. The crucifixion of Jesus: a saving event?

By far the most significant pericopes are Mark
10:42-45 and 14:22-25. Mark introduces the former para-
graph with a dialogue between Jesus and the sons of Zebe-
dee, who want the seats to the right and to the left of Jesus
reserved for them in the coming kingdom (10:35-37). Jesus
then predicts his own and the two disciples' martyrdom using the metaphor of a "baptism to be baptized with." The
same image appears in Luke 12:50,[98] in the context of a
prediction of the coming "divisions" even within families
because of decisions for or against Jesus (12:51-53/Matt
10:34-36 Q). Since the misunderstanding of the disciples,
who are more concerned with self-aggrandizement, regular-
ly follows each prophecy of the suffering of Jesus,[99] Mark
may have formed this introduction himself using a traditional metaphor of Jesus and probably also a tradition of the
martyrdom of James and John.[100] Anyway, the dispute ex-
pands in v.41, comprising now of all of the twelve. After

stating the radical difference between the "great men" in the world and the really great ones in his own group (42-44) Jesus concludes: "For the son of man also came not the be served but to serve and to give his life as a ransom for many."[101] This is reminiscent of the servant of the Lord in Is 53 (v.12: the servant of the Lord "poured out his soul to death" and "bore the sin of many"),[102] which would have been obvious to any pious Jew of that time.

Did Jesus himself say these words? Luke leaves this passage out of his gospel, but includes a very close parallel in 22:24-27, also starting with a dispute between the disciples about which of them would be the greatest. The context is here the last meal and this may be an earlier tradition than the one in Mark.[103] Is this also true for the wording in Luke 22:27: "I am among you as one who serves"? The answer is very difficult. First, *diakonein* ("to serve"), which is also used in Mark 10:45, is typical of the language of the church. It is lacking in the Greek Old Testament, but there are a few passages, in which *diakonos* ("servant," especially serving at table) appears.[104] However, *diakonein* may easily render the Hebrew verb 'bd, which is frequently used in the Hebrew Bible, and is translated by *douleuein* in Is 53:11. The verb *diakonein* is also found in Luke 12:37, which is one of the most amazing sayings of Jesus: "Blessed are those servants whom the master finds awake when he comes; truly I say to you, he will gird himself and have them sit at table, and he will come and serve them." What master on earth would act in this way? This is very typical of the parables of Jesus.[105] I am, therefore, inclined to hear Jesus' own voice in both sayings, Luke 12:37 and 22:27, though Luke may have hellenized the style. I would even ask whether the preference for the term *diakonein* in the early church is not due to the fact that it was used in the first translations of the sayings of Jesus that describe his own ministry in this way. Thus it is quite possible that Mark 10:45 is authentic, though Luke 22:27 seems to me to be even more probably so.[106]

The problem of the second text (the last supper) is similar. Two main versions exist: a) Mark 14:22-25, which has two parallel statements about Jesus: "This is my body" and "This is my blood of the covenant poured out for many"; b) 1 Cor 11:23-26, with a different structure: "This is my body for you" and "This cup is the new covenant in my blood." Again, the wording in Mark offers a more semitic sound than that found in Paul, but the more parallel forms are usually later than the less parallel, as there is a trend to make more clearly parallel sentences. John 6:53-56 seems to presuppose a text like "This is my flesh"/"This is my blood,"[107] followed by some promise of eternal life. Be this as it may, whenever I ask somebody to quote the words of Jesus at the last supper, he or she always quotes a version which is much more parallelized than any text in the New Testament, because our liturgies have combined various texts so that the two words about the bread and the cup run in almost total unison. Besides, if Mark's text were prior to that of Paul (whose letters were written down almost two decades before the Gospel of Mark), we would expect "flesh" as the contrast to "blood," since in Hebrew as well as in Greek literature it is almost exclusively "flesh" that is connected with "blood."[108] Therefore I think that the Pauline tradition is closer to what Jesus said than the Markan one, though there is no evidence in Jesus' preaching of the idea of the new covenant, except in Mark 14:24 and 1 Cor 11:25. Nor do we find there a clear reference to Jer 31:31. The background seems to be rather "the blood of the covenant" which Moses "threw upon the people," before going up to the mountain with the seventy elders "to eat and drink" in the presence of God and in an upper world "like the very heaven" (Ex 24:8-11).

There is also an apocalyptic flavor in both traditions. In Mark the words about the bread and cup are followed by the prediction that Jesus will drink wine anew in the kingdom of God, which seems to be authentic. 1 Cor 11:26 adds, probably in remembrance of this or a similar apocalyptic saying, that in the Lord's supper the church "proclaims the Lord's death until he comes." Matthew repeats the Markan text, adding "for the forgiveness of sins" after the phrase "poured out for many." Luke prefaces the words about the bread and cup[109] by a double prediction that Jesus will eat the passover lamb and drink wine again in the kingdom of God.[110]

The result is similar to the case of Mark 10:45/Luke 22:27. In spite of its semitic style, the substance of the Markan tradition seems to be posterior to the Lukan or Pauline variants. *Dogmatically,* the latter is less fixed to a clear identification of the bread and cup with the body and blood of Jesus, as the act of Jesus as savior was still more open to different interpretations in Luke 22:27. This fits the way Jesus used to speak about the mystery of God's presence on earth in his parables (and otherwise).

Whether Jesus actually used the words of 1 Cor 11:24-26 or of Mark 14:23-25, or maybe still some other version (for instance, the special tradition of Luke 22:15-20), it is the *body* of Jesus, not his flesh that is mentioned. Furthermore, the blood of Jesus is never connected with the wine, but with *the cup*, which prevents the misunderstanding of a magical transformation of substances.[111] Moreover, it is pertinent to notice that all three variants agree in three main points. First, Jesus interprets in his words the *common eating* of bread (and the passover lamb, Luke 22:15-16) *and drinking* of the cup. Second, he does so by interpreting his *gestures of giving* his disciples the bread and the cup (or at least by pointing to the passover lamb that they will eat presently). Third, Jesus speaks of the "many" or of the disciples, *for whose sake* these gifts are given, though this remark is connected to the first word in Paul's liturgical passage, and to the second in the gospels. It might have been lacking in the special tradition of Luke, though not in the present Lukan text as a whole. As to the content of the three reports, the emphasis varies, but they all (Luke in the full text of 22:15-20) point back to the *death of Jesus*, underline *the covenant character* of this meal for the present church and proclaim *a future fulfillment*.

Even if we were very critical, it would be difficult to deny that Jesus emphasized in some memorable way his last meal with the disciples, and that he showed, at least by his gestures of offering them bread and wine, that it was meant as a gift for them, even beyond his own death.[112] If not before, at least on the evening of his last day on earth, Jesus delivered a message to his disciples—again perhaps it was more through his actions than in explicit words—that even his death should be understood, as also his whole ministry, as God's gift for them. That the last meal was nothing but the last meal—an everyday meal not differing from other meals, which was only retrospectively recognized as the last one with Jesus, as Crossan suggests[113]—is almost unthinkable. It is reported as a very specific meal by Paul, Mark and a special tradition of Luke. Paul writes in the early fifties that he received this tradition "from the Lord" (1 Cor 11:23). He must have known how the church in Antioch celebrated the Lord's supper, three years after the death of Jesus at the latest[114] He spent two weeks with Peter and James in Jerusalem only two or three years afterwards.[115] Would they all have told him that this was the way Jesus instituted that supper on the last day of his life, if it had not been so?

So was Jesus' death a saving event? What is the answer? Up to now, we have seen that Jesus must have reckoned with a critical confrontation when he went up to Jerusalem and then directly into the center of the opposition—into the temple. Death from his enemies was a real threat and everything points to the conclusion that he reflected upon this possibility.[116] On the last evening, at least, he must have distinguished this final meal from all the former table-fellowships by his acts and very probably, also by some words of interpretation. We cannot be sure of exactly what he did and said, but in my view the general picture of these days and of that last evening is reported in a reliable way by the synoptic gospels. They are buttressed by another text in which, for me, the voice of Jesus is unmistakable. It seems to have no connection with the question as to how Jesus looked upon his coming death, but I think that an examination of it may well be very helpful to confirm, and perhaps to modify, the general picture of this last period in the ministry of Jesus.

4. *The parable of the compassionate father (Luke 15:11-32)*

Rudolf Bultmann defined "myth" as the act of expressing the other-worldly in worldly thought, and the divine in earthly language.[117] This is exactly what Jesus did when he told his parables. By his introductory phrase "The kingdom of God is like..." and by the choice of his stories, he avoided any misunderstanding that he wanted to give a definition of God—or the acts of God—or a direct description of heaven. Scholars have rightly argued that in this parable there is no place for a redeemer figure; there is only the father and his sons—God and the sinners and no mediator between them. *If* this parable were merely an illustration of a dogmatic doctrine of salvation—if Jesus were but a rabbi who wanted to teach (by using some more popular illustration) the way in which salvation would be possible—this would be true. But this is not what Jesus tried to do.[118] What then was his intention?

In all his parables, Jesus tries to bring "the divine" —God and the life and rule of the kingdom of God—down to people on this earth. He tries to convey to them that other dimension of reality which cannot be directly expressed in earthly language. But it can be reported in pictures, metaphors and parables, which evoke earthly, human experiences. They open the ears and eyes, the heart and all the senses to an experience which runs parallel to them and yet goes far beyond them. Only in this way does the other-worldly reach into a worldly language and those who "have ears to hear" begin to hear. Therefore it is not a doctrinal description of salvation that is given to us in this parable, which we can then possess from now on and keep for ever. But rather, a story is given to us and starts to live in us. It is the story of a human experience in which God is living and ruling and behind this picture the mystery of God becomes visible. Jesus claims the authority to draw this picture, because he identifies himself with his message. He does not merely tell his parable, he lives it. Who else would dare to do so? Who else would know his heavenly father so intimately (as his "abba") that he could tell such a story?

The parable starts with the father and it ends with the father, and the father is the only one on the stage in both halves of the story. Whereas the two sons follow step by step the course that is to be expected,[119] the father acts in an absolutely unexpected, surprising way.[120] By telling this story, Jesus brings God into our lives: "A father had two sons." Indeed, God has very different children. "The younger of them said: 'Father give me the share of property that falls to me.'" He acts as if the father were already dead. In some way, he has, like Oedipus, already removed his father from his life—and "killed" him.[121] "Thus, he divided his living between them." Not one word of protest! The father could have said: "I had to wait until my father was buried and you will have to do the same"! He could also have said: "If you need some more pocket money, okay." He could have proposed to leave the son the interest of his future share and then to see what he would do with it. The father has the power to speak in this way, he is omnipotent in his house. But the father forgets all these rules for the sake of his rebelling son. And this one "went into a far country and there squandered his property." He went as far away from his father as he could! That "a great famine arose in that country," was not his fault, but forced him "to join himself to one of the citizens, who sent him to feed his swine," which is for a Jew, of course, the worst place imaginable. The youngster looked for a substitute father who, as often happens, proved to be a very hard father. And the real father? He possesses still all the power necessary to fetch his son back, to go himself, to send a friend or to ask the police to do so. It is only his love that hinders him from doing so. And yet it is that same father that moves his son to return: "My father has bread enough and to spare." Sure, it is the bread, not the love of his father that entices him; yet, it is the bread of the *father*. Whether he really repents or simply plans to win his father with good words, we do not know. The Bible says merely, in a matter-of-fact way: "he came to himself." The reaction of the father, however, is totally unexpected: "While he was yet at a distance, his father saw him and ran and embraced him." This omnipotent father could well have waited at home, humiliating his rebelling son in order to make him, eventually, truly humble. But *this* father's heart was obviously always with his son, looking out for him; he "ran" towards him—though any old man in the Orient would rather step along with dignity, not betraying how glad he was to see his son back. And he "embraced him" without any words, any sermon on repentance or grace, almost sacramentally. And when the son started his confession, his father cut him short, not allowing him to say "treat me as one of your slaves," as he had made up his mind to do in v.19. There waits for him instead a festive meal with all that the heart desires. The father at the head of the table, his son beside him, food and drink, music and dance. Is this the correct and final portrait of this omnipotent father?

It is, but we cannot capture him in one image. Five minutes later, he is out in the darkness and the cold, where he might catch pneumonia. His elder son came home from his labor (typical for him), and got angry—music and dance even before sunset! And "he refused to go in" and said to his father: "When this son of yours came..." No longer does he speak of him as his brother, and no longer is *this* father

his father. He shows indeed that he has killed his real father
long ago. He served only the picture of his father, as he
himself created it: his father as he should be. He even flings
his indignation into his father's face: "This son of yours has
devoured your living with harlots." The story says nothing
of that; it is only the fantasy of the elder son that paints this
picture, maybe because he himself would wish to do so.
And this omnipotent father, who could have called his servants to drag his son into the banquet hall within five minutes, does not force anything, because he still loves his son.
For love is about the only thing that cannot be forced upon
anybody. If I am authoritarian enough I can compel my
child to kiss a visiting aunt, but if I do the child will probably be put off loving her for ever. So nothing is left for
this father except a heart burning with love and a few
words, not rebuking, but simply stating: "Son, you are always with me and all that is mine, is yours." This is the
truth: "You *are* with me—all *is* yours." The question is
only whether his son can hear it or not.

      This would be mere fairy tale if it were not Jesus
who told it. With such a parable filling out his whole existence he goes up to Jerusalem. This picture of God accom-
panies him. If his claim to be authorized to tell the story of
God's love was not unfounded, he was living himself his
parable. He was still living it when, a few weeks later, he
was hanging on the cross, totally powerless, not able to
move his hands or feet, no longer having one square inch of
soil to stand upon. Is this really the son of that omnipotent
father? Indeed, he is: "Do you think I cannot appeal to my
father and he will at once send me more than twelve legions of angels?" (Matt 26:53).[122] But his father has decided
to love his lost sons to the end; therefore Jesus goes—
taking the side of his father— to his death. Like the father
at the end of the parable, Jesus has nothing more than his
heart burning with love and a few words inviting those who
are around to come: "Father, forgive them, for they know
not what they do"—"Truly, I say to you, today you will be

with me in Paradise"—"Father, into Thy hands I commit my spirit" (Luke 23:34,43,46). In Jesus the unimaginable love of the father in this parable has come true. Its open end points to the cross of Jesus and puts the question to the hearer as to whether he hears the message and sees this love, so that it might also reach him.

5. *The explicit soteriology of the early church*

When Jesus went up to Jerusalem, he had no illusions. People "are evil," though they "know how to give good gifts to their children" (Luke 11:13)—whether they belong to the "type" of the younger or of the older son. And Jesus knew that God is love; so much so that God cannot and will not force them to come home, but can only wait and suffer with them until they are ready to come. It is this unimaginably loving father of whom he spoke to all those who listened to him, and with whom he sided for good. How far, and in what way, he explicitly interpreted his readiness to risk his life and his decision to take suffering and death upon himself, we are not sure. However, if we are not stretching our criticism too far, we could scarcely doubt the well supported tradition that—at least at the last meal with his disciples—Jesus explicitly spoke of his willingness to die in obedience to the will of God for the sake of the "many."

After Easter, the church had to put that understanding into retrospective language. It did so in two ways. On the one hand, it told the story of the passion of Jesus. This was so important that, in contrast to all other traditions, the main structure of this story is the same in all four gospels. In our earliest gospel, in Mark, the report of Jesus' last week covers 18 pages, whereas 32 describe his whole ministry prior to this week. On the other hand, the church devised formulas that summarize the content of the faith of the church in terms of his death and/or his resurrection. We shall investigate them on pp. 74-75.

Jesus' death on the cross was a shock for the early
church. From the flight of the disciples (Mark 14:50) up to
later texts like 1 Cor 1:18-25 or Luke 24:19-21 this is still
visible. Even after Easter, it was not easy to cope with this
fact. It is astonishing that as far as we can see, the early followers of Jesus did not yield to the temptation to forget this
embarrassing death and to proclaim only the victory of
Easter and the lordship of the exalted Christ. Two approaches towards a solution of the riddle of this shameful
death can be detected in our traditions.

One of them is the way in which they told the story.
In Mark it is done in a language that reminds the reader of
various Psalms which tell of the suffering of the righteous,
without really quoting them. This is the case in Mark
14:18,34; 15:24,29,34,36 (Ps 41:9; 42:6; 69:21; 22:18,8,2;
69:21). It seems to have happened more or less unconsciously, the author neither referring directly to the scriptures nor repeating them literally. Reflection on these passages is seen in the later gospels though. Matthew (27:34)
adds to Mark 15:23 that the wine offered to Jesus was
"mingled with gall," because Psalm 69:21 (22) speaks of
"gall" and "vinegar." Vinegar is mentioned in Mark 15:36
(Matt 27:48), but not gall. The letter of Barnabas emphasizes that "gall and vinegar" was given to Jesus to drink and
deals at some length with this fact and its importance for
the believer. John 13:18 and 19:24 mention explicitly the
fulfillment of Ps 41:9 and 22:18. They also illustrate this by
reporting that Jesus gave Judas a morsel of bread (13:26)
and that the soldiers under the cross did not merely "part
the garments," but also "cast lots," as the Psalm says, because "the tunic was without seam" and should therefore
not have been cut in pieces. Other scriptural passages have
been detected. Matthew inserts in 27:43 a new verse of Ps
22 (v.9): "He trusts in God, let God deliver him now, if he
desires him; for he said 'I am the son of God'." This is very
interesting, because it reflects, especially in its last sentence, the picture of the suffering righteous one, as it is

painted in Wisdom of Solomon 2:10-20 (and then in 4:16-5:5, cf. p. 86). This comes closer to what has happened to Jesus than anything else in pre-Christian Jewish literature. It speaks of suffering, of a violent death and of vindication by God through exaltation to the ranks of the sons of God and his saints (the angels), from where the suffering righteous one appears to his former opponents, who are terrified by his appearance and repent. This "poor righteous one" (v.10) "calls himself servant (or child) of God" (v.13) and boasts of God being his father (v.16), so that his enemies say: "If he is son of God, God will care for him" (v.18).

Following this line of interpretation, the solidarity of Jesus with all the suffering righteous ones in Israel is seen as the center. Jesus shares and *fulfills* their destiny. This is rightly understood as the solidarity of God with the suffering people of God. Nobody who knew anything of the ministry of Jesus could misunderstand this as a solidarity only with those who were righteous according to the standards of the moral or religious rules of that time. Luke, for instance, paints the contrast to such a view in the picture of Jesus' solidarity with "the criminal who was hanged railed at him" (23:39-43).[123] This leads to a development in soteriology whereby salvation becomes a reality as the believer is included within Jesus' life and death and resurrection. Of course, this view is already pictured during the earthly ministry of Jesus in the discipleship of those who followed him. After Easter, it was more his death and resurrection that came alive in the death of the old existence of each believer and in the creation of a new and eternal life "in Christ." "One has died for all, therefore (*not*: they who believe in him are spared dying, but) all have died" (2 Cor 5:14). "We were buried with him in baptism into death, so that, as Christ was raised from the dead..., we too might walk in newness of life" (Rom 6:4).[124] "...that I may share his (Jesus') sufferings, becoming like him in his death, that ... I may attain the resurrection from the dead" (Phil 3:10). And in a pre-Pauline hymn: "Christ Jesus ... emptied him-

self taking the form of a servant, being born in the likeness
of men ... and became obedient unto death, even death on a
cross" (Phil 2:7-8). This view became most important in
Paul's emphasis on "living in Christ," which is based on
Paul's conviction of a change in lordship: "If we live, we
live to the Lord, and if we die, we die to the Lord. Whether
we live or whether we die, we are the Lord's. For to this
end Christ died and lived again, that he might be Lord both
of the dead and of the living" (Rom 14:8-9).[125]

Following the other avenue of approach, Isaiah 53
turns up as the background text. As with the parallels to Jesus as the suffering righteous one, this again does not start
with a theologically reflected identification. The title "servant of the Lord" (or: of God) appears, with the exception
of an Old Testament quotation in Matt 12:18 (and there in
the context of Jesus' healings, not of his suffering), only in
Acts 3:13-26 and 4:27-30. But Mark 10:45 and 14:24 seem
to be rooted in that chapter, and also for the formula in
Rom 4:25 this connection should not be doubted (cf. also
Rom 10:16; Matt 8:17; Luke 22:37; Acts 8:32-33). This interpretation centers around the idea of expiation or atonement. But in its later development very different forms of
understanding come to the foreground. First, Paul connects
atonement with reconciliation. This term comes from a totally different background—namely from the Hellenistic
view of two armies or countries at war, whose ambassadors
(2 Cor 5:20!) try to establish peace.[126] The New Testament
never uses the term in the sense that God should be reconciled; it is, without exception, always humanity who has to
be reconciled to God. Second, the rite of bringing a sacrifice is sometimes clearly influencing the language of the
New Testament (cf. Rom 8:32; 1 Cor 5:7 and especially
Hebrews 9-10). But a sacrifice was, in the Old Testament,
never a payment for guilt. "A pair of turtledoves" are never
equivalent to the firstborn son (Luke 2:23-24)! It is rather a
sign of the grace of God, who accepts such a small gift instead of the son, and of the gratefulness of the parents.

Third, the act of salvation is often expressed in the pattern of substitution without any religious overtones, as far as the picture goes (cf., for instance, Rom 5:6-8). Other linguistic variants are the image of paying a "ransom" to liberate somebody, for instance a slave, or "cleansing by washing" (Eph 5:26; Tit 3:5).[127]

Therefore any exclusive theological model of an interpretation of Jesus' death and its meaning for the believer—for instance tracing all these statements back to the pattern of expiation by a sacrificial death—can become wrong. All our explicatory words are pictures and it depends on the context and on what the speaker has experienced as to whether they convey the truth of what has happened or not.[128]

The parable of the compassionate father which Jesus told said nothing at all about the death of a son for the sake of his brothers and sisters. But if Jesus had not forgotten his own parable—and how could he have done so?—he knew that the children of his heavenly father are rebellious children, and also in Jerusalem. And he knew that his place was with the father at the end of his parable, lovingly waiting—not calling down the twelve legions of angels—but ready for the worst—without even stopping to love the rebels. This is what the church understood and this is the real center of all that it tried to express in its theologically reflected stories, formulas and statements.

V

JESUS THE RESURRECTED

In Chapters Two and Three we have seen that Jesus did not proclaim the kingdom of God without using parables or significative actions. Chapter Four showed that in all probability, Jesus reckoned with a possible attack by his opponents in Jerusalem—which could even cost his life— yet he expressed his willingness to take this upon himself, at least on the last evening, by his words and/or his gestures. These results of historical research must be expressed at different levels of certainty—on a higher level for Chapters Two and Three, and on a lower level for Chapter Four. But what do these results mean?

1. *The necessity of "mythological" language*

In the first case, historical research can show that the parables in the tradition of the words of Jesus are not introduced or followed by a statement that summarizes the message of the parable in direct informational language. The few exceptions look suspiciously like being later redactional additions of the early church. The question is whether this parabolic language is used out of necessity, or simply because Jesus liked to speak in this way, maybe merely because of his rhetorical preferences. That is to say—does this finding show that there are dimensions of reality that cannot be conveyed in a language without imagery? The answer to this cannot be given on the exclusive basis of historical methodology. It seems to be a logical conclusion, but it cannot be proved. It could also be that Je-

sus—or we as the readers of his parables—simply imagine
that such dimensions exist and therefore speak in such
forms. Even less can we prove that Jesus was right when
speaking of these dimensions as "the kingdom of God," and
as it being the reality behind all the historically provable re-
alities.

When we do accept this extra dimension of reality,
we do so on the ground of our experiences. Just as we find
it inadequate to speak of love, of art, or of music merely by
using a language of logical and provable information, so
also with regard to our experiences of God. We need a language that evokes, by its imagery, experiences in us—the
joy of love, the impression of an object of art, the emotion
of music. We need it even more when speaking of God and
our encounter with God. Out of necessity we must express
"the unearthly" in earthly terms,[129] that is, in a "mythological" language. As K. Niederwimmer once wrote,[130] our sub-
conscious life, which is more important than the rational
one, expresses itself in "myths." Even Bultmann, in his famous program of demythologization,[131] emphasized that we
should not *remove* the mythical statements of the New Testament, but *translate* them into existentially meaningful
terms for those who—no longer lighting oil lamps—switch
on the electric light and expect as a matter of course that
the electric current causes the bulb to shine.[132] This illustration of his was wide open to misunderstanding, as if all
mythical terms should be reduced to mere rational expres-
sions. What we can and must do is to translate the mytholo-
gy of the first century into that of the twentieth. For instance, to speak of "transcendence" instead of "heaven" is
not less "mythological" (or "parabolical") than "heaven." It
expresses the picture of "going beyond" (the rationally con-
ceivable world?), which is exactly what the Latin *transcen-
dere* means. But the term has won, in the long discussions
of the philosophers, a certain "band-width" within which
the meaning of the word is to be detected. It is better pro-
tected against misunderstandings to the left and to the right

than the old term of "heaven" (which is mixed up with the idea of the sky). Nonetheless, it does not provide a simple definition which we could take over without getting involved ourselves in re-examining our existence. Thus we may think that this term or that term in the mythological language of the New Testament is no longer appropriate and that we have to look for a better (still mythological) phrase, but find that we cannot do without this kind of language. "Resurrection" is such a mythological term. What are the facts behind the resurrection of Jesus?

2. *The resurrection of Jesus: the facts*

The resurrection of Jesus is nowhere *described* in the New Testament. We find the first account in the apocryphal gospel of Peter, in what is definitely a later development of the tradition.[133] Just as human eyes cannot see God, so too they cannot see the miracle of the resurrection. This statement is true, whether it is understood in terms of what really happened on Easter morning, or to the truth of which the authors of the tradition were convinced.

The facts open to historical investigation are as follows. *First,* the disciples of Jesus despaired on Good Friday[134] and yet were ready—very probably not more than seven weeks later at Pentecost[135]—to proclaim Jesus as Lord and even to go to prison and to die for him. This definite and profound change in the lives of the disciples is a historical fact.

A *second* historical fact is the way in which the group of disciples and those who joined them after Easter reacted to what had happened. It is surprising how much importance they attached to the events connected with the death of Jesus and his appearing as the living one after Easter. In section 3, we shall deal with the reports of these appearances, but before we do so we ask what, according to

the earliest traditions, was the center of the belief of those
who were forming themselves as the early church.

On the one hand, traditions of his earthly ministry
and sayings of Jesus were handed down and developed, as
we have seen in Chapter Three when dealing with the parables and the history of their tradition (p. 32). There existed
collections like Q—or later the gospel of Thomas—that
concentrated on the sayings of Jesus. Yet it was the passion
story that was first given a fixed structure and in our earliest gospel, Mark, the story of Jesus' passion covers more
than a third of the whole gospel (Cf. p. 66). Here as in the
other three of our gospels, the crucifixion of Jesus and his
resurrection form the climax towards which the narrative
aims. Mark closes his gospel with the message of the resurrection of Jesus given by the angel and probably, with a
hint towards the creed of the church.[136] The other three gospels tell various appearances of the risen Lord to his disciples.

Even more important are the short formulas by
which the church summarized its faith that we find in the
New Testament. The earliest ones, it seems, contain the fact
of Jesus' death[137] or of his resurrection[138] or of both
events.[139] Probably later, but still before Paul wrote his letters in the early fifties, we also find summaries that combine these events with the coming of Jesus from God[140] and/
or his exaltation to God to become Lord over his church or
even the world.[141] A pre-Pauline Jewish-Christian formula
combines Jesus' descendance from David with his installation as son of God by his resurrection (Rom 1:3-4), and a
pre-Pauline hymn speaks of his pre-existence with God, his
"emptying himself" to "being born in the likeness of men,"
his "death on a cross," his exaltation and lordship over all
the powers "in heaven and on earth and under the earth"
(Phil 2:6-11).[142] However these creeds may have developed,
and whatever the earlier and the later stages may have
been,[143] it is clear that the "frame" of Jesus' life—his origin

in God's world, his saving death, his resurrection and exaltation—was more important than his earthly ministry, which is scarcely mentioned in these formulas (maybe in Phil 2:7-8 and in 2 Cor 8:9, explicitly in Luke's summaries in Acts 2:22 and 10:38-39). I think that an account of the ministry of Jesus has also been given to the Hellenistic communities (cf. besides Phil 2:7-8 and 2 Cor 8:9, also 1 Cor 11:23; Gal 4:4), but as far as we can still detect the belief of the early church in these formulas and hymns, Jesus was not (or at least not primarily) seen as a charismatic leader and teacher, whose program could be taken over independently of his whole existence and destiny. It was not the ideas and doctrines that he brought which were central for the early church, but he himself—his divine origin and authority, his death and resurrection, his exaltation and lordship without end.

As historians we can only say that this has been the belief of that early church; we cannot decide whether this was the right understanding of Jesus and his ministry or a misunderstanding. On pp. 51-52 we saw that what Jesus claimed to be in his preaching and his actions, was at such an unusually high level that it manifests either his religious mania or the very truth. He lived, spoke and acted as if the very being of God were present in his life, his preaching and his work, fulfilling all the promises from the creation of the world on, now and here. As if? Or was it, indeed, exactly what happened? This is what the early church believed: that in Jesus' coming from God, in his devotion to his heavenly father and to his earthly brothers and sisters up to his death, in his resurrection and exaltation, God had become present indeed in our world, bringing final salvation to humanity. Here we cross the borderline between historical research and faith. Whether we say "yes" or "no" to this belief is a matter for our personal decision.

A *third* historical fact is the text of 1 Cor 15:5-8. Paul has "received" the tradition that he "delivered" to the

Corinthians "as of first importance" (or: "first of all").
Whether its origin lies in Antioch or Jerusalem, it is unthinkable that its content would differ in any essential point
from what Paul heard in both churches, very soon after the
death of Jesus.[144] He is quoting at least up to v.5: "...that
Christ died for our sins in accordance with the scriptures,
that he was buried, that he has been raised[145] on the third
day in accordance with the scriptures and that he appeared
to Cephas, then to the twelve." Two main sentences speak
of Jesus' death and resurrection, predicted in the scriptures
and confirmed by Jesus' burial and his appearances respec-
tively . V.6 starts a new sentence in a different style and includes a personal remark of Paul, while in v.8 he speaks of
himself in the first person. Hence it is fair to conclude that
vv. 6-8 no longer belong to the quoted tradition, but have
been added by the apostle.

The appearance of the risen Jesus to Cephas and the
twelve[146] is reported in the quoted formula. The phrase *ophthe* with the dative (literally: "he was seen to...," not: "by"!)
is used in the Greek Old Testament around ten times[147] in
the context of appearances of God to various persons. It always marks the beginning of a word of God to them. All
emphasis is laid on God being the subject of a free act of
revelation, whereas the motif of being seen by the addressees is not especially underlined, sometimes not even mentioned besides the choice of the word *ophthe*.[148] In the case
of 1 Cor 15:5-8 there is no doubt that in the understanding
of Paul, Jesus was seen indeed by the witnesses of his resurrection and that this was essential: "Am I not an apostle?
Have I not seen Jesus the Lord?" (1 Cor 9:1). In the same
way, Mark 16:7; Matt 28:17; John 20:18,20,25,29; Acts
9:27; 22:14 (equivalent to *ophthe* with the dative in 9:17;
26:16) use the verb in the active mood and prove that the
moment of seeing the risen Lord was essential.

Cephas is mentioned in particular. The same is true
of Mark 16:7. Luke 24:34 even runs: "The Lord has risen

indeed, and has appeared to Simon," without mentioning
the twelve. This seems to be a traditional formula, in which
the conclusion "the Lord has risen indeed," central for the
faith of the church, precedes the information about what
has happened to Simon and has led to this new certainty.
Within the story of the two disciples returning from Emmaus it forms a kind of anti-climax; they hastened to return
to Jerusalem and are cut short by this report. Though there
is no narrative of this appearance to Peter in the New Testament,[149] it is well rooted in the tradition and is not to be
doubted that he had this experience as the first of the
(male![150]) disciples. Of the twelve, Paul knows some, if not
all. In Gal 1:18-19 and 2:9, he mentions explicitly Cephas
(and "James the Lord's brother"), whom he saw at his first
visit and John at the second. Moreover, Gal 2:2 presupposes a meeting with the whole community in Jerusalem and
another more private one with its leaders.

When we look at the additional names in vv.6-8,
Paul is, of course, an eye-witness of his own experience
near Damascus. An appearance to James is described, without any historical reliability, in the gospel to the Hebrews.[151]
Paul also knows him personally. "All the apostles" must be
a group larger than the twelve, including also female apostles, as Rom 16:7 shows.[152] Paul apparently knows some of
them. Finally, he knows that some of the "more than five
hundred" to whom the Lord appeared have died, though
most of them are still alive.

It is, in my view, a fair conclusion from this testimony that all these persons whom Paul knew personally (or
at least he knew some of them in the larger groups) were
convinced that they saw the risen Jesus Christ.[153] With this
conclusion we have reached about the limit of what we can
say historically. Everything else is, historically speaking,
open to question.

3. *How did the disciples see the risen Lord? The stories of the gospels*

In 1 Cor 15:8 Paul considers his experience equivalent to those of other witnesses of the resurrection. He therefore uses the same term "appeared to me." If there is any truth in the tradition of Acts 9:3-9,[154] Jesus appeared to Paul from heaven. In Mark 16:7 the angel predicts that Peter and the twelve will see the risen Jesus without giving any details. According to Matt 28:16-20, they saw him on a mountain in Galilee. But the only word that suggests that Jesus himself is on the mountain, is "coming" (in the sense of "approaching them") and this is used by Matthew over fifty times in his gospel, usually even in the same grammatical form and often introduced redactionally into his Markan tradition. Moreover, Jesus begins his address to the disciples by telling them: "All authority in heaven and on earth has been given to me." Hence we may assume that in the tradition which Matthew reports here, Jesus spoke to them from heaven in a way similar to how he spoke to Paul, according to Acts 9. This is different from what we read in all the other stories, in which he meets his disciples on earth, walking and eating with them, even letting himself be touched by them. Is all of this only later redactional embroidery? If Matthew possibly altered his tradition, has the same happened in all the other texts?

When we ask *where* these appearances took place, Paul gives no indication at all. The first one happened according to (Mark and) Matthew in Galilee,[155] according to Luke and John in Jerusalem on Easter Sunday evening (Luke 24:13,33,36; John 20:19). Luke reports no appearance in Galilee, but John 21 describes how the risen Lord met his disciples, who are fishing as if nothing had happened, later in Galilee. These events cannot be harmonized. Possibly the eleven disciples saw Jesus first in Galilee, which moved them to return to Jerusalem, to the center of Israel, where they saw him again, perhaps more than once.

Mark and Matthew would then have been interested only in the first event which proved the fact that Jesus had risen, Luke and John only in the later ones, which became important for the continuation of the Jesus-movement in the mission of the disciples. This would not exclude the possibility that some—for instance the two who walked to Emmaus and first of all, the women—saw Jesus in or near Jerusalem earlier or at the same time as the eleven in Galilee.[156] But again, it is not clear what happened historically and in what sequence.

This is also true in the case of the *women*. All four gospels report their visit to the tomb which turned out to be empty. One (John), two (Matthew), three (Mark) or many (Luke) of them come to the tomb,[157] see an angel rolling away the stone (Matthew) or find the tomb already open. The angel sitting on the rock (Matthew), a young man in the tomb (Mark) or two men (Luke, cf. John 20:12) tell them that Jesus has risen and that the disciples will see him in Galilee (Mark and Matthew). Luke, who includes no story of an appearance in Galilee, changes this information to an admonition of Jesus, to "remember what he told you while he was still in Galilee." In John there is no commissioning by the angels, but Peter and the beloved disciple check the open tomb, *before* Mary of Magdala meets the angels.[158] Jesus himself also appears to the women (Matthew) or to Mary of Magdala (John). About the only thing all four gospels agree upon is the fact that the women were the first bearers of the message of the resurrection of Jesus.

No doubt there is a tradition behind the first report in the gospel of Mark. Since the list of the women in 16:1 differs from that in 15:40 and still a different one in 15:47, and since the variants of the synoptic parallels are more striking in the Easter stories than in the story of the women observing the death and burial of Jesus, we may conclude that the background tradition of Mark 16:1-8 has also been handed down independently from the passion story.[159] But a

definitive historical reconstruction is impossible. This is
closely connected with the problem of the open and empty
tomb.[160] Even if we do not take John 20:3-10 into account
(which states that Peter and the beloved disciple investigated the tomb and found it empty) the story has no clear fea-
tures and varies even within the synoptic tradition. It is not
mentioned anywhere outside of the gospels . Anyway, our
texts convey no unambiguous answer, even to the question
whether the women (or at least one of them) saw the risen
Jesus and whether they brought the message of the angel(s)
to the eleven or not.

4. *What happened in Galilee, Jerusalem and near Damascus around 30 A.D. ?*

For Lüdemann the first appearance to Peter was a
vision or, more accurately, a hallucination of intrapsychic
origin, which was a part of the mourning process. There are
modern reports of such visionary and sometimes also auditory experiences.[161] This first vision was infectious and trig-
gered all the other appearances, even to the "more than five
hundred." Evidence of mass-visions, brought about by a
first individual vision, exists in history.[162] This hypothesis
cannot be disproved, but it has to be discussed.[163]

First, the evidence for such visions, especially for
mass visions, should be carefully sifted. This is a task still
to be done. In the examples listed by Lüdemann, a central
message by the one who is seen seems not to be part of the
reports. For Paul, it was the center of his experience.[164]
Some of those hallucinations listed by Lüdemann happened
to persons that were dozing. Not one of the Easter experiences is dated at night, let alone in a dream. Most of them
are "isolated" experiences at various places and dates, and
not connected with other stories as their beginning or continuation.[165] It is therefore very difficult to imagine that a
solitary first vision created a general enthusiasm and
caused, in an "infectious" way, more and more people to

see the same thing. It is also difficult to imagine this process, because it does not answer any obvious conscious or
unconscious yearning or nostalgia of the visionary, at least
not primarily. In the New Testament, Paul is the first who
connects the resurrection of Jesus with the resurrection of
the believer at the end of the world. This is not found in the
pre-Pauline tradition of 1 Cor 15:5(-8) or anywhere in the
stories of the gospels or in the early formulas of the
creed.[166] The experience of an appearance of the risen Lord
was not primarily a guarantee for eternal life, but on the
contrary, a call to serve him even in the law-courts and in
prison and if necessary, in losing one's life. *This* was, originally, the context of the message of the one who was seen
by his disciples.

Second, Paul clearly and definitely distinguishes his
experience near Damascus from "visions and revelations"
like the one of which he tells in 2 Cor 12:1-6. These should
never be communicated to others. Only "speaking as a
fool" could he mention it, forced by the addressees of his
letter (11:21; 12:11). In contrast, "seeing the Lord" was the
basis of his apostleship (1 Cor 9:1; Gal 1:15-16) and he presupposes the same for all the apostles (1 Cor 9:1). Therefore Paul never uses the term *horama* ("vision" as in Acts
9:10: the Lord speaking to Ananias; 16:9-10: a man of
Macedonia to Paul; 18:9: the Lord to Paul privately; but nowhere connected with the Easter events). Conversely, he
does not speak of having seen the Lord in the visions and
revelations of 2 Cor 12:1-10.[167] Appearances such as the
ones listed in 1 Cor 15:5-8 no longer happen: "Last of all
he appeared to me," and in twenty years since then nobody
else has experienced another one. It is not only Paul that
says so. The function of the tradition of Jesus' ascension is
exactly the same. Luke—perhaps afraid of false teachers
who boast with new revelations (Acts 20:26-32)—fixes the
period for the appearances of the risen Lord at 40 days. The
fact of a definitive limit is important, whereas the dates giv-
en for it still vary for centuries in the tradition of the

church.[168] The remark in John 21:14, which emphasizes that
the coming of the risen Lord to his disciples in Galilee was
"the third time that Jesus was revealed to the disciples after
he was raised from the dead," combined with the final
statements of this chapter, are also a part of the process
which fixed a final limit to these revelations. As far as we
can see, in the early church the events of 1 Cor 15:5-8 are
strictly distinguished from the on-going voice of the Holy
Spirit and all other visionary and auditory experiences connected with it.

Third, Lüdemann identifies the appearance to the
"more than five hundred" with the distribution of the Spirit
at Pentecost (Acts 2:1-13).[169] This is rather improbable. On
the one hand, all the marks of an Easter story are lacking.
Nothing is said of any appearance of the risen Lord, and
surprisingly enough, not even of a mission of the disciples
to proclaim the gospel in Israel or in the world, as we find
in Matt 28:19-20; Luke 24:47-49; Acts 1:8 (also implicitly
in Mark 16:7 par. and John 20:17,22-23) and in the list of
those who were called to become apostles in 1 Cor 9:1;
15:5-8. On the other hand, the coming of the Spirit is prom-
ised, but not recounted in the Easter stories, with the exception of John 20:22-23, which is most likely a more developed form of the saying in Matt 18:18 and/or 16:19.

Fourth, has there been any mass hallucination that
has so influenced the course of history for centuries? Usually they have been experiences of ecstasy which have pe-
tered out rather quickly. I am aware of the importance of
the tradition of the whole ministry of Jesus, which certainly
stood behind the Easter experiences. All the same, the question has to be asked as to whether these remembrances
could really explain the mission of the disciples and its
enormous challenge to—and influence in—the world.

Fifth, the problem of the revelation to the women at
the open and empty tomb is much more difficult. The dif-

ferent reports vary greatly. It is certainly not to be expected
that an overwhelming experience like that could have been
told with the precision of a police-protocol; emotions were,
of necessity, out-weighing rational observations. Nonetheless the historical question of what actually happened, is
not easy to answer. Form-criticism shows that the motif of
not finding the corpse of the deceased belongs to the stories
of an exaltation without a death (Elijah: 2 Kings 2:16-17;
Moses: Deut 34:6). Lüdemann discusses this hypothesis of
an exaltation of Jesus from the cross without an actual
death.[170] There is no doubt that the exaltation of Jesus to his
Lordship is important in the New Testament. Phil 2:9
speaks of exaltation only, not of resurrection.[171] But
Lüdemann sees rightly that in the New Testament it was always the exaltation of the *crucified* Jesus, whose death was
never questioned.

One might add that it is not very likely that the story
of the empty tomb could have been created for apologetic
purposes—to prove the resurrection—for it is a story in
which only women appear as witnesses. Though they are
mostly better observers than their male partners, they
would scarcely have been accepted in this role in the world
of first-century Judaism. The insistence of the New Testament on the resurrection of Jesus "on the third day" could
also be explained by the detection of the empty tomb on
Sunday morning as a decisive sign of this fact.[172] The
weight of these arguments should be considered, but they
are certainly not enough to *prove* the empty tomb as a historical fact.

However, one point is clear. Wherever the women
are mentioned, they are said to have been at the tomb of Jesus. One name is common to all the stories (including the
death and burial of Jesus): Mary of Magdala. In the fourth
gospel, she is even the only visitor to the tomb (before she
fetches Peter and the beloved disciple). We might conclude
(I think with some probability) that some revelation must

have been granted to the women at the tomb, or at least to one of them. We may also agree with C. H. Dodd: That "diese Perikope auf undefinierbare Weise etwas wie aus erster Hand an sich hat." ("I cannot for long rid myself of the feeling [it can be no more than a feeling] that the *pericope* has something indefinably first hand about it.")[173] Paul might well have left out this event in 1 Cor 15:5-8 because it was not combined with the question of leadership in the church and legitimation as a preacher[174] and/or because the testimony of women was not accepted in Jewish law. In this case, Mary of Magdala (with or without companions) would have been the first witness to the resurrection of Jesus. Concerning this, or at least concerning the fact that the women were the first ones to bring the message of the angel about Jesus having been raised, we cannot say more than "might," or perhaps "probably." Historical certainty is not given by our texts.

To sum up, what we can know with a strong measure of historical probability is: (1) that there was a definite change in the lives of the disciples, a change that created a spiritual movement spreading through the whole Roman Empire and then through Europe and the world, going on for centuries; (2) that the church traced from the very beginning the origin of all this back to the centrality of the cross and the resurrection of Jesus; (3) that all those listed in 1 Cor 15:5-8 were convinced they had seen the risen Jesus; (4) (with less clarity) that the women received some revelation at or near the tomb.

Could all this be due to some hallucinations? Is there not a much simpler and more probable answer: that God has raised Jesus indeed[175] and that he was the cause of these events and still is? I may add that in my view we should not be so reluctant to concede the existence of very concrete and visible traces that an event like the resurrection of Jesus left within our earthly sphere.[176] It is not so important though to know exactly what "miracles" have happened, or which appearances occurred and which did not, as long as there is no doubt that it happened within our history, at a specific time and place.[177] Does this mean we are left with a mere "maybe" or is there a stronger basis for our belief in the resurrection of Jesus?

5. *Back to the earthly Jesus*

Did Jesus say anything of his coming resurrection during his earthly ministry? This is not to be expected, since he was never interested in teaching doctrines about God or the Spirit or the messiah—or about resurrection. How could he have argued for what was still a future event? As a Jew he would have believed in his resurrection or, at least in a kind of life after death, because he certainly did not belong to the Sadducees. But we can say more. It is in my view impossible to exclude all the references to the future from the authentic sayings of Jesus—all the warnings against a final rejection and all the promises of a final consummation—which are often expressed in parabolic language. These sayings are also always clearly related to his preaching and ministering (words *and* healings, table-fellowship, calls to follow him, etc.) in the "here and now."

There is *Luke 12:8-9* (Q): "I tell you, everyone who acknowledges me before men, the son of man will acknowledge him before the angels of God; but he who denies me before men will be denied before the angels of God." There is a similar saying in Mark 8:38; thus this word is attested in two independent sources. In the form it occurs in Luke it is an offensive and an ambiguous statement. Who is this "son of man"? Someone other than the "I" of Jesus? Or does Jesus identify himself with him? The much smoother form of Matthew avoids this ambiguity and replaces both the "son of man" in the first half and the passive construction in the second half of the saying by the "I" of Jesus. Crossan thinks that the original version contained in both parts merely the "divine passive": "...will be ac-

knowledged...will be denied" and that it was Luke who introduced the son of man, because this term was already in
the Markan word (8:38/Luke 9:26).[178] But the old methodi-
cal rule that the smoother, better understandable form is
usually a later correction of a more awkward and less understandable one, has to be applied to this word too. The
Lukan form is typical of Jesus who challenges his hearers
by not giving them doctrines or titles they can simply parrot
after him, but rather asking them to answer his challenge
themselves and in their own language. At the same time, it
is a form that fits the situation. Whenever we are to express
really significant feelings or experiences in words, we often
try to speak in a modest and guarded way. Paul acts in exactly the same way and changes his "I" to a third person
term, speaking of a "man" (in semitic terms: "a son of
man"!), when telling of his astonishing vision of the heavenly world: "I know a *man* in Christ who...was caught up
into Paradise...and he heard things that cannot be told,
which man may not utter. On behalf of *this man* I will
boast, but on *my own* behalf I will not boast, except of my
weaknesses" (2 Cor 12:2-5). There are quite a few other examples of this way of speaking.[179]

Could Jesus also have spoken in this way? There is
no doubt that he was at home with sapiential language and
theology. The proof of this are the many wisdom sayings in
the sermon on the mount, for instance. This is the context
(the *Sitz im Leben*) of that picture of the suffering righteous
one, of whom we spoke on p.68. He calls himself the son of
God, but is tortured recklessly by his opponents and shame-
fully killed, but then exalted to the heavenly world. Of him
we read that he will testify against them, "and they will be
terrified and moan: "We have derided him and considered
his end shameful; why is he counted among the sons of
God and why is his lot among the holy ones?" (Wisdom
5:4-5).

In Luke 12:8-9, Jesus pictures himself similarly as

the decisive witness (for the defense or for the prosecution) before the court of God—not as the judge of the last day,[180] but the witness before the "angels" in the Lukan version, before Jesus' own "father in heaven" in the Matthean one. In this way, I think, Jesus expected his final vindication and his future role. This, of course, implies his resurrection from the dead, though without any clear indication as to when it would take place, immediately after his death or at the last day.

If we exclude the predictions of his death and resurrection by Jesus himself,[181] there is only one pericope in which Jesus deals with the general question of the resurrection: *Mark 12:18-27*. The first part contains a rather silly argument of the Sadducees—which could have been a problem arising out of a discussion with the Pharisees—and an answer by Jesus, which would have been very widely accepted in his time. V.26 is a new beginning, leading from the question as to *how* we can imagine a life after resurrection to the other question whether there is a resurrection at all. Thus, vv.26-27 are very probably an independent unit, appended redactionally to vv.18-25. The answer of Jesus is very simple. According to the scriptures, God is the God of Abraham, of Isaac and of Jacob, and God is not a God of the dead, but of the living. Resurrection faith is as simple as that. When God enters into a covenant with a person, God—who will never cease to live—enters the life of that person. Therefore the experience of the living God who proves to be stronger than all kinds of needs and adversity, will not end in death. God has given himself to a living, not to a dead Abraham, Isaac and Jacob.

This is exactly how Israel learnt to believe in resurrection. Israel is an amazing example within the history of religions. It is a nation that for centuries, without belief in any better life after death, believed and trusted in God fervently and faithfully in a surprising way. The theory that religion is only due to a projection of our own wishes and

hopes, could be verified almost everywhere except in Israel's first centuries. Yet Israel experienced this living God,
this presence and help, not only in good times, but even
more in illness, in failures, in defeats, in the destruction of
the nation, of Jerusalem and of the temple and in the resulting exile. It experienced God's never-ending presence and
help also in apostasy and sin. Hesitantly, Israel learnt during and after the exile, to conclude that God's presence and
help would not end in death: "When my soul was embit-
tered, when I was pricked in heart, I was stupid and ignor-
ant, I was like a beast toward you. Nevertheless I am con-
tinually with you; you hold my right hand. You guide me
with your counsel and afterwards you will receive me to
glory" (Psalm 73:21-24).

    All this, of course, is an argument only for the gen-
eral resurrection of the dead, and not for a specific resurrection, as happened to Jesus on Easter day according to the
New Testament. Nevertheless, it is *Jesus* who thus affirms
resurrection—the one who claims that God is living, speaking, working in his ministry in a unique "eschatological"
way, fulfilling all the experiences of Israel and therefore
also working in his death and resurrection.[182] It might be
that the church in its very early period understood his resurrection in this "eschatological" way: as the beginning of all
the end-events, of the definitive coming of the kingdom of
God and of the resurrection of all the dead.[183] Be that as it
may, the way Jesus argued in Mark 12:26-27 and the way
Israel learnt to believe in resurrection is also the way the
followers of Jesus learnt to do so. An outstanding example
is John 11:17-30, dealing with an event within the earthly
ministry of Jesus, but written retrospectively in the time after Easter. Thus it was shaped by post-Easter experiences,
rather than containing literally authentic words of Jesus.

6. *The explicit soteriology of the Johannine church:* *John 11:17-29* [184]

This pericope is not the protocol of a dialogue between the historical Jesus and a historical Martha. It is shaped and even created by the experiences of a disciple of Jesus after Easter. Of necessity, it uses "mythical" language; without it we could never speak of resurrection. It is the message of the risen Jesus which "oozes" out of the experiences of the disciple. There is no "one hundred percent pure" Word of God. Water distilled to one hundred percent purity no longer quenches the thirst. It must flow first through the soil and absorb its minerals and even its mud. So also the Word—it must, for instance, absorb the grammatical rules of the Hellenistic language of that time, a tongue saturated by Biblical and mundane rhetoric, and also the slang phrases and antique conceptions of that world. Most of all, it must flow not only through all the concepts of the first up to the twentieth century, but also through those of our personal lives. Otherwise, it would remain mute (cf. above, pp. 71-73).

The dialogue starts in John 11:17-18, explicitly in the geographically and chronologically fixed situation of times gone: Bethany near Jerusalem and four days after the death of Lazarus. Yet it is a situation that we might meet in much the same way. A beloved person has died and "many of the Jews had come to Martha and Mary to console them." This is what we may do too. Shared helplessness and misery is better than nothing, it might even be really helpful, but it does not change the predicament. Into this situation Jesus comes. And "Martha said to him: 'Lord, if you had been here, my brother would not have died.' " Very often this is what we think and say: "If..." and it is always looking back and an exercise in fantasy: "If I had been able to go to school, if I had married that one, if I had chosen another profession." But Martha is a pious Jewess: "And even now I know that whatever you ask from God,

God will give you." What an almost limitless faith, for which we might envy her. Yet when Jesus answers her: "Your brother will rise again," she postpones her expectations to the last day, to another world, to some far away religious, transcendent reality: "I know that he will rise again in the resurrection at the last day." Perhaps we might struggle to say this, at least with such certainty. Yet what is the basis of her belief? Probably what her parents told her, what her friends believe and especially, what a conservative rabbi taught her in her religious instruction in the synagogue. We may be like her, more or less, grateful to parents and teachers and friends who conveyed real values to us. We may be vague in our views of a life after death, perhaps curious about what will come to us then, as a famous agnostic philosopher of our time said, perhaps not even that. But in a situation like that of Martha, it may not be of first importance whether our preconceived ideas are orthodox, agnostic or atheistic. It might even be that a person far away from any religious hopes could be more open to the unexpected message of Jesus than another one who thinks that she or he knows what eternal life will be like.

"Jesus said to her: 'I am the resurrection and the life.' " The resurrection and true, eternal life are meeting Martha now, not only after her death. They are present, ready to enter her life and to merge with it. When the author of the fourth gospel wrote this down, Jesus was for him already the risen Lord, as he is for us. Therefore he speaks out of his experience of this Lord. There were times in his life (as there are in ours) in which he was sure that he was guided on his way, not by human influence and not by his own will and plan. Perhaps he too prayed and was sure that his prayer had been heard (though perhaps not in the way he had expected) rather than vanishing into thin air. Perhaps he too had the experience in which a word of God in his Bible or in a talk with a fellow-man or woman had hit him, warned him, consoled him, changed him. Whenever something of this kind happens, a life of another dimension, the life of God himself enters our biological lives. Then God starts to form and to build up a new personality, in everyone of us in a different and unique way. And this life of God cannot die; what God has built may be forgotten by us, may be hidden under all kinds of other experiences, but it cannot die—just as God cannot die: "Whoever lives and believes in me, shall never die." Of course Martha will die biologically, as we will and all our psychological and physical troubles, and this is very well so. But the Martha (or whatever our name may be) that God has started to build, will not die: "He who believes in me, though he die, yet shall he live." Her body will vanish and also the portraits that the rabbi may paint at the funeral and that her family and friends may keep in their memories. But still living is that life of God, which Jesus has brought to her, so that it merged totally into her human life in a mixture of shame and joy, of forgiven sins and simple manifestations of gratitude, of hope and love. This personal life with God, unique in its specific form, will find its perfection when God will create for her a new "spiritual body" (1 Cor 15:44) from all these fragments. Jesus asks her: "Do you believe this?" And Martha has really understood. She knows that something much more than merely a new doctrine is at stake; she answers: "Yes, Lord, I believe that you are the Christ, the son of God." The basis of her belief in a present life of resurrection and also in a coming resurrection after death, is her personal relation to Jesus, a man from Nazareth, in whose words and deeds—in whose way of living and dying—God has come to her. She might not be able to express this in dogmatic terms, but she knows that she speaks, in her fumbling and very simple words, of a new reality. How well she understood what Jesus said to her becomes clear in the narrative: "When she had said this, she went and called her sister Mary, saying quietly: 'The teacher is here and is calling for you.' " And Mary "rose quickly and went to him." In this story Martha detected her real life. She "found herself." But with Jesus, this is never the final goal, because we cannot reach this "wholeness of life" without all the others who are living with us. We find ourselves only when becoming open to Jesus and thus to other people. There is no "I" without a "Thou" and, therefore, also a "she" and a "he."

The word of God is never of a one hundred percent purity, since it flows, of necessity, through the soil of our experiences. First of all through that of the first disciples and then of the authors of our New Testament. But since the question "What do we really know of Jesus—who was he?" turns, again of necessity, into the other question "Who is he—for these early Christians and especially for us?" it must also flow through the soil of our own experiences. Thus it is that academic teachers and New Testament students also become, whether they want to or not, always preachers—grateful to, or critical of, what these Biblical authors preach.

VI

CONCLUSIONS

On pp. 15-16 I sided with Käsemann and Barth against Bultmann and voted for taking the historical basis of faith seriously. Since God's Word comes to us in human words, in the Hebrew and Greek texts of our Bible, it would be foolish to proclaim that we could dispense with learning Greek and Hebrew and with using all the philological tools the philologians can give us. This understanding of the words of the Bible and the historical facts it describes is surely no *guarantee* that we will hear the voice of God in them, but without such an understanding we could not hear it at all in the Bible. There is a deep truth behind what Pedro Casaldalgia[185] says: "Betrachte die Sterne, Abraham, versuch nicht, sie zu zählen" ("Contemplate the stars, Abraham, do not try to count them"). Yet even here, trying to count them might at least convince me that there are so many that their number goes beyond all my imagination.

After the investigation above of our texts and the historical problems they raise, I drew conclusions far less skeptical than those of Bultmann. I have argued that the central data of Jesus' ministry, his death and his resurrection appearances are reported in a trustworthy way by our texts. But in another way, the results of our investigations are striking, perhaps even paradoxical. On the one hand, Bultmann, who was so extremely skeptical of any reconstruction of the life, death and resurrection of Jesus as a foundation for faith, was convinced that the fact of the crucifixion (his famous "that" i.e. that Jesus had been crucified) and resurrection of Jesus (as he understood it: into the kerygma) was indispensable for Christian faith.[186] On the other hand, Casey, Crossan, Lüdemann and others who have helped so much towards making such a reconstruction do not seem to consider it a necessary foundation for belief in Jesus as the *Christ*. Therefore, the real problem to be discussed is the 'extra nos' ('outside of us') of the reformers. How is it to be interpreted?

For Bultmann it was the axiom, presupposed as the basis for all his arguments, that God had acted in Jesus' crucifixion and resurrection so that the justification of the believer face to face with God became a reality, long before we ever heard about it. Hence whether we consider much of what we read in the New Testament and especially in our gospels, to be historically trustworthy, or only a little (as Bultmann did) is perhaps not of primary importance, though it is important enough to get as much clarity about it as possible. Even for Bultmann it was absolutely essential to know, beyond the mere fact of the crucifixion, that it was *Jesus* who was crucified and proclaimed as the savior of the world—not any criminal or lunatic—and to know, at least in a general way, who this Jesus was. The really basic problem is, therefore, what we mean when we say that God became flesh in Jesus.

Do we mean that in the life, the death and the resurrection of Jesus (even if we reduce it to what Bultmann tells us) God or, even more precisely, *the grace of God*[187] has definitively accepted us as the children of God ("eschatologically"—to use the language of Bultmann) and that this is not dependent on all the ups and downs of our faith (Gal 4:4-7)? Or does it merely mean that all we know of Jesus, is and remains true "outside of us," but only becomes a reality for us, as far as we let ourselves be influenced by it,[188] in exactly the same way as would be true of the writings of Plato or Shakespeare?

That I vote in favor of the former sense has become clear, I hope. But again, what does this mean? On pp. 32-34, I tried to understand Jesus as *the* parable of God.[189] As far as it concerns God's act, this is true for all humanity, whether they believe it or not, and whether they say so or not. But this leads to two final questions: *First*, if this is so, is the religion I adhere to irrelevant? At this point, I can only offer a very personal answer. If I see it correctly, the fact that "the Word became flesh" (John 1:14)—that God became a human being as an infant dependent on his mother for every mouthful of milk and every change of diapers, and as a man rejected and executed on a cross like any criminal—is without real parallels in the history of comparative religions. A sign of this uniqueness is the fact that the social question has only arisen in countries that have been influenced by Jewish-Christian traditions. So God's hard and unshakeable love can nowhere be detected better than in Jesus Christ. Therefore, I should tell Christians and non-Christians about him. But I should never think (not even unconsciously, I hope) that as a Christian I would, of necessity, live any nearer to God than a non-Christian. The last day might very well reveal that I knew Jesus and could study the New Testament for many years, but that the lives of some Buddhists (or whatever their religion was) were closer to Jesus (whom they did not know) than mine.[190] We shall all see the face of God only then (and I think it will actually be the face of Jesus) and we shall all be redeemed only by the love of God that became flesh in Jesus. Thus my knowledge of Jesus does not elevate me above the non-Christian, though it is an invaluable gift of God for my whole life here. Nor does the ignorance of others degrade them or place them beneath me. God's judgment may be even harder over me than over those who had no chance to know Jesus.

Second, does this mean that all people will finally be saved—even those who knew Jesus, but neglected or rejected this knowledge? Is God's grace so overwhelmingly strong that it prevails even against our weak, our non-existent, or our wrong beliefs?[191] Does it mean that whether I think of God and live with God well—or not so well—or badly—or even not at all, God *has* become a loving father and a loving mother (Is 66:13) for me and remains this forever? With these questions we reach a threshold that we cannot cross. There are words like Rom 2:5-8: "By your hard and impenitent heart you are storing up wrath for yourself on the day of wrath when God's righteous judgment will be revealed. For he will render to everyone according to his work...," cf. also Matt 25:31-46. And there are other words like Rom 11:32: "God has consigned all people to disobedience that he may have mercy upon all" (cf. also Luke 15:31 or John 8:7). We need both the strict warnings against all our lazy indifference and/or our pig-headed opposition, together with the promise of God's grace in Jesus Christ, which is by definition stronger than we are and all our failures. If, however, we thought we knew how God will reveal himself in the last judgment, we would be putting ourselves above God.[192]

At this point, we can only close in the same way as J. S. Bach headed every one of his compositions: S.D.G, "Soli Deo Gloria" ("all honor to God alone").

NOTES

CHAPTER I

1. Cf. D. M. Smith, *Johannine Christianity* (Columbia, SC: University of South Carolina Press, 1984), 191: "What is latent in the Synoptics is patent in John."

2. John P. Meier, *A Marginal Jew. Rethinking the Historical Jesus I* (New York: Doubleday, 1991), 25.

3. *Die Geschichte der Leben-Jesu-Forschung,* (Tübingen: Mohr, 1906).

4. R. Bultmann, *Exegetica* (Tübingen: Mohr, 1967) 469. The following section is a summary of what was important for me in his lectures in Marburg (1932-1935). His ascertainment of an implicit christology in the preaching of Jesus is to be found now in his *Theologie des Neuen Testaments* (1st edition, 1953), 8th edition, ed. O. Merck (UTB 630, 1980), 46.

5. "Neues Testament und Mythologie," in: *Offenbarung und Heilsgeschehen* (München: Kaiser, 1941), 27-69; originally published as vol. 96 of Beiträge zur evangelischen Theologie, 1941, 7-64 (same publisher). Further discussion is summarized in P. J. Achtemeier, *An Introduction to the New Testament* (Philadelphia: Westminster, 1969), 55-70 (esp. 56-63); English literature, *ibid.,* 169-171.

6. Implicitly already in F. Buri, "Entmythologisierung oder Entkerygmatisierung der Theologie?" in: H.W. Bartsch (ed,), *Kerygma und Mythos* II (Hamburg: H. Reich, 1952), 85-101, esp. 90, 96-98 (cf. 99: myths necessary for a special kind of self-understanding); and explicitly in H. Braun and D. Sölle (see below, notes 9-11).

7. "Das Problem des historischen Jesus," in idem, *Exegetische Versuche und Besinnungen* (Göttingen: Vandenhoeck u. Ruprecht, 1960), I, 187-214.

8. SBT 25 (London: SCM, 1959).

9. *Jesus* (Stuttgart: Kreuz-Verlag, 1969).

10. Idem, "Der Sinn der neutestamentlichen Christologie," *ZThK* 54 (1957): 368-371, "Die Problematik einer Theologie des Neuen Testaments," *ZThK* 57, (1960): 18.

11. *Stellvertretung: ein Kapitel Theologie nach dem "Tode Gottes"* (Stuttgart: Kreuz-Verlag, 1967), 175-181, 190-192. Cf. M.

Machovec, *A Marxist Looks at Jesus* (Philadelphia: Fortress, 1976), 88-93; F.Belo, *Das Markusevangelium materialistisch gelesen* (Stuttgart: Alektor, 1980), 318-324, 353-354. More detailed references in E. Schweizer, *Jesus Christ—the Man from Nazareth and the Exalted Christ*, (Macon, GA: Mercer University Press, 1987) (London, 1989), 16; idem, "Jesusdarstellungen und Christologien seit Rudolf Bultmann," in: B. Jaspert (ed.), *Rudolf Bultmanns Werk und Wirkung* (Darmstadt: Wissenschaftliche Buchgesellschaft, 1984), 122-148.

    12. *Paul and Palestinian Judaism, 1977; Paul, the Law and the Jewish People, 1983; Jesus and Judaism*, 1985 (all published by Fortress Press, Philadelphia). To the general topic, cf. J. H. Charlesworth (ed.), *Jews and Christians* and *Jesus' Jewishness* (New York: Crossroad, 1990 and 1991). For the very important development after 1985 cf. G. Boccaccini, "Middle Judaism and its Contemporary Interpreters (1986-1992)," *Henoch* (Torino) 15, 1993, 207-233.

    13. Meier (as in note 2), 258-262.

    14. I am happy to see that J. Neusner as a Jewish rabbi agrees definitely on this point (R. J. Hutchinson, "What the rabbi taught me about Jesus," *ChrTo* (1993, Sept.13): 29.

    15. *From Jewish Prophet to Gentile God* (Cambridge: Clarke, 1991) (my review *ThLZ* 117 [1992]: 353-356).

    16. J. D. Crossan, *The Historical Jesus* (San Francisco: Harper, 1991).

    17. Mark 1:16-20, Crossan, 408-409. Cf. p. 48 below.

    18. Cf. pp. 50-51, below.

    19. Crossan, 293-294. Cf. below p. 49 and note 71.

    20. Though Crossan 449 (cf.434 and xxiv-xxv) traces the *core* of Luke 15:11-32 back to Jesus, the parable plays no role in his book. Cf. below pp. 62-66.

    21. Crossan, 350-351.

    22. Crossan, 390-394.

    23. Crossan, 397-398, 410-411.

    24. Crossan, xxxi-xxxiv.

    25. Crossan, 383. E. Hennecke/W. Schneemelcher, *Neutestamentliche Apokryphen* (Tübingen: Mohr, 3rd ed., 1959), 202-222, dates the manuscript at the turn of the 4th to the 5th century and the last redaction of the text around 140, early 3rd century at the latest, since it is used in the Acts of Thomas; several synoptic sayings are already combined and there are very few words which you could seriously consider as authentic words of Jesus.

    26. Against Crossan (385-387) cf., Joel Green, "The Gospel of Peter: Source for a Pre-Canonical Passion-Narrative?" *ZNW* 78, (1987): 293-301. He answers the question negatively: the gospel of Peter is no independent witness. G. Lüdemann, *Die Auferstehung Jesu*, (Göttingen: Vandenhoeck & Ruprecht, 1994) (English translation expected from London: SCM, 1995), 160, note 507, thinks that the author of the Gos-

pel of Peter knew all four Gospels (though they were not yet canonized).

27. Against Crossan, 385-387. Cf. also note 88 below.

28. Crossan, 328.

29. Klaus Wengst, "Barnabasbrief," TRE V, 238-241, dates it between 130 and 132 (16:3-4 pointing to the building of the temple of Jupiter and no hints of the war of 132-135).

30. E. Schweizer, *A Theological Introduction to the New Testament* (Nashville: Abingdon 1991/London: SPCK 1992), 47-54; regarding the chronology of Paul's life cf. note 34 below. Skeptical about the existence of a Q-community is also J. Halverson, "Oral and Written Gospel: A Critique of Werner Kelber," *NTS* 40 (1994): 189-190.

31. Crossan, 329.

32. Crossan, 250-251.

33. So Crossan, 361, cf. here pp. 59-61. A review of Crossan's book by Ben F. Meyer appeared in *CBQ* 55 (July, 1993): 575-576.

34. Gal 1:18-20. The stay of Paul in Corinth can be dated because Gallio (Acts 18:12) was proconsul there from Spring 51 to Spring 52 (or, less probably, one year later). Counting back from that date, we come to 32-33 A.D. (35 at the latest) for the calling of Paul. Cf., for instance, E. Schweizer (as in note 30), 55-56; Lüdemann (as in note 26), 57-58; J. Murphy-O'Connor, "Paul and Gallio," *JBL* 112, 1993, 315-317.

35. K. Niederwimmer, *Jesus* (Göttingen: Vandenhoeck & Ruprecht, 1968), cf. here p. 72 and note 130.

36. Crossan, 424-425.

37. To be honest: I am not sure about the letter of Jude, for instance. But I shall not vote for removing it from the New Testament, and even if some synod should ever decide to do so, it would merely be a marginal correction.

CHAPTER II

38. Meier (as in note 2), 167-177.

39. Cf. the forthcoming book of B. W. Henant, *Oral tradition and the Gospels*, JSNT, Suppl. X2.

40. Meier, 178-183. For the limited value of form-criticism and its crisis, cf. E. Schweizer, "Karl Ludwig Schmidt—Abschied von Illusionen über Jesus und die Kirche," *ThZ* (Basel) 47, (1991): 195-196.

41. Meier, 184-195.

42. Cf., e.g. H. Weder, *Die Gleichnisse Jesu als Metaphern*, FRLANT 120, 1978, 11-57, and the (mainly British/American) literature quoted in E. Schweizer, *Jesus Christ* (as in note 11), 86, note 50

43. Cf. Bill. (index s.v. "Sauerteig"): many rabbinical references; H. Windisch, article "zyme," ThWNT II, 904-907; also J.A Fitz-

myer, *The Gospel according to Luke*, AncB 28A, 1985, 954-955.

44. A. Jülicher, *Die Gleichnisreden Jesu* (Freiburg: Mohr, 1888), e.g. 147-148 (first ed.).

45. J. D. Crossan, *In Parables* (New York: Harper and Row, 1973), 13.

46. Fitzmyer (as in note 43) 1019: 3 times "a peck and a half" = 40.8 liters and, as I measure, one liter is equivalent to around 625-650 grams of flour.

47. Crossan (as in note 16) 350-351, and Jülicher, (mildly criticized in my dissertation *EGO EIMI*, FRLANT 38, 1939, 114, note 11).

48. L. Beirnaert, "La parabole de l'enfant prodigue (Luc 15,11-32) lue par un analyste," in: F. Bovon/G. Rouiller (ed.), *Exegesis*, (Neuchâtel/Paris: Delachaux et Niestlé, 1975), 136-144. Eng. edition, Pickwick, 1978.

49. Fitzmyer (as in note 43), 1087.

50. Weder (as in note 42) 58, with A. Wilder, R. Funk, D. O. Via, J. D. Crossan, N. Perrin. For the following example cf. E. Jüngel, "Metaphorische Wahrheit," in P. Ricoeur/E. Jüngel, *Metapher* (EvTh Sonderheft), 1974, 73.

51. See pp. 71-73 below. By "mythological language" I do not, of course, mean "fairytale" language, but a language that dares to speak of a truth not detectable, measurable or verifiable by scientific tools like photographs, repeatable experiments (whenever someone wants to check them) and so on, which is nonetheless not merely *a* truth, but the *central truth*.

52. There is in the text of Paul an emphasis on the personal aspect of this equivalence. After having shown in repeated statements that what is in the view of the world folly and weakness, is, in the view of God wisdom and power, and that the world's wisdom and its wise men are foolish for God, he reminds the Corinthians that God chose them, who in the judgment of the world are foolish and weak, low and despised, and actually amounting to nothing. We would expect the apostle to go on: " . . . so that you now become wise and righteous and holy." But this is not what Paul writes; he continues in a totally unexpected way: "God made *Christ Jesus* our wisdom, our righteousness and sanctification and redemption."

CHAPTER III

53. As Crossan, (as in note 16), 351, also notices.

54. E. Schweizer, *The Good News according to Mark* (Louisville: John Knox Press, 1970, London: SPCK, 1971), 383-386; expanded: *Das Evangelium nach Markus*, NTD 1, 5th-7th ed, 1978-1989, 214.

55. Matt 9:27-34 reports the healings of two blind men and of

a deaf and dumb man, which are doublets to the stories in 20:29-34 and 12:22-24. Matthew has to include them already at this point because these healings are mentioned in 11:5 as having happened already.

56. There are two inclusions: "Blessed..." in 11:6 corresponds to 5:3-10 and the phrase about Jesus "healing every disease and every infirmity" in 4:23 is repeated literally in 9:35 and also, regarding the disciples, in 10:1. The promise to them in 10:7-8 actually takes up what 4:23; 9:35 (and 11:5) tell of Jesus.

57. This is buttressed by Matthean redactional additions in 22:39-40 (loving one's neighbor is equally as important as loving God, and: "On these two commandments depend the law and the prophets.") Matthew has also introduced the commandment to love one's neighbor in 19:19 and the desire of God for mercy, not for sacrifice in 9:13 and 12:7.

58. 1 Cor 12:9; James 5:14-15; Acts, etc. Cf. the polemic against Jesus (and his church) in Mark 3:22; Matt 9:34; 12:24; Luke 11:15.

59. P. J. Achtemeier, "The Origin and Function of the Pre-Marcan Miracle-Catena," *JBL* 91, (1972): 200-202.

60. G. Theissen, *Urchristliche Wundergeschichten*, StNT, (1974): 142-143.

61. Cf., for instance, M. Trautmann, *Zeichenhafte Handlungen Jesu. Ein Beitrag zur Frage des geschichtlichen Jesus* (Würzburg: Echter, 1980), 267.

62. See Fitzmyer, (as in note 43), 922. The word is also attested in the Gospel of Thomas 113 (cf. 3:1 and Crossan, [as in note 16], 283).

63. Cf., for instance, Fitzmyer, 1159-1162; I. H. Marshall, *Commentary on Luke*, NIC (1978), 655; against the translation "among you": H. Riesenfeld, "Le reigne de Dieu, parmi vous ou en vous? (Luc 17,20-21)," *RB* 98, (1991): 190-198.

64. Käsemann, (as in note 7), 210.

65. Also Crossan, (as in note 16), 352.

66. Cf. p. 9.

67. Crossan, (as in note 16), 261-264.

68. Also in the Gospel of the Ebionites, fragment 1. In Q, the only call of Jesus to follow him is Luke 9:59/Matt 8:22. The group of the twelve is, however, presupposed in Luke 22:30/Matt 19:28 (and in 1 Cor 15:5).

69. Cf. e.g. Matt 8:22; Mark 10:21; Luke 14:33; John 12:25-26. The problem of the narrower and the wider circle of followers of Jesus is well discussed in J. Roloff, *Die Kirche im Neuen Testament* (GNT 10), (1993): 42-46.

70. Arguments for authenticity: J. Roloff, "Anfänge der soteriologischen Deutung des Todes Jesu (Mk 10:45 und Lk 22:27)," NTS 19, 1972/73, 38-64. Cf. pp. 58-59.

71. Though parallels to all the petitions of the Lord's prayer are found in the Judaism of Jesus' time, the concentration of these few is for me a sign of authenticity, cf. p. 10 and note 19.

72. It is used without the definite article in Dan 7:13 and consequently Rev 1:13; 14:14 ("like a son of man"). Cf. Schweizer, *Jesus Christ*, (as in note 11), 45-49, more recently: D. R. A. Hare, *The Son of Man Tradition* (Minneapolis: Fortress, 1990); M. Casey, (as in note 15), 46-55 and 150. 'The son of man' turns up also in the gospel of the Hebrews 8 (Hieronymus, *Vir. inl.* 2), "*filius hominis*," in a word of Jesus; and furthermore, in the Coptic gospel of Mary 8:18-19 and 9:9-10 (here in a question of the disciples), cf. R. McL. Wilson, "The New Testament in the Gnostic Gospel of Mary,' *NTS* 3 (1956/57): 241-242. Both gospels belong to the second century A.D.

73. Cf. only Mark 9:41; 12:35; 13:21 (in the parousia, not in Luke 17:23); Matt 23:10; John 17:3; cf. E. Schweizer, "Jesus Christus," TRE XVI, 722 and 714 for "son of man."

74. Idem, "Der Menschensohn," *ZNW* 50, 1959, 185-209, also in my *Neotestamentica* (Zürich: Zwingli, 1963), 56-84. Cf. summaries in *JBL* 79, 1960, 119-124 and *NTS* 9, 1963: 256-261, contrariwise A. Vögtle, *Die "Gretchenfrage" des Menschensohnproblems*, (Freiburg: Herder 1994), especially 43-45.

75. Hare, (as in note 72), esp. 257-282; Casey, (as in note 15), 46-55, 150; Crossan, (as in note 16) esp. 248-249, 255. Cf. p. 13 above.

76. I also suggested in 1959 (cf. note 74) that Jesus expected to be not the judge, but the decisive witness (for prosecution or defense) in the last judgment, cf. Luke 12:8-9 and pp. 85-87 with note 180 (against Crossan, 254).

77. E. Fuchs, *Jesus—Wort und Tat* (Tübingen: Mohr, 1971), 96: "Jesus surrenders his own person unprotected to the comprehension of the hearer" (my translation). Gospel of Thomas 91: "They said to him: Tell us who you are so that we may believe in you"—but Jesus does not do so!

78. Cf. also my article "Jesus Christus" in TRE XVI, 721-725.

CHAPTER IV

79. Most recently, cf. G. Lüdemann, (as in note 26), 58, including note 170, against various hypotheses of a merely apparent death of Jesus, for which there is no evidence at all.

80. Ann. 15.44: Auctor nominis eius Christus Tiberio imperitante per procuratorem Pontium Pilatum supplicio affectus erat.

81. Ant. 18.63-64.

82. Ant. 20.200.

83. Other relations to Jesus played a role in the early church,

for instance a cousin of Jesus (Eusebius, church history III 11; IV 22.4—here Hegesippus is quoted).

84. This is difficult for the Roman Catholic church. "Brother" is occasionally used for a cousin, etc., but it is unthinkable that so many different authors always used that word in its wider sense and never the correct term (cf. Col. 4:10). It would be *possible* that Jesus' brothers came from a former marriage of Joseph, if he was a widower when marrying Mary. For the protestant churches the other children of Mary are no obstacle.

85. Probably 30 A.D. All gospels agree that Jesus was crucified on a Friday, which was, according to the synoptic authors, the passover day, but according to John 18:28; 19:14 (very probably historically correct) it was the day of preparation; cf., for instance, Lüdemann (as in note 26), 209.

86. E.g., H. Schürmann, *Jesu ureigener Tod* (Freiburg: Herder), 2nd ed., 1975, 65.

87. Mark 8:31; 9:31; 10:33-34 and parallels, also Luke 17:25.

88. Crossan (as in note 16), 393-394; Lüdemann (as in note 26), 60-64: the name is traditional in Mark already, but the act of burying Jesus is not historical. The extreme skepticism that alleges that the passion story is an exclusively literary creation of Mark (cf. above p. 11 and notes 27-28) goes back to W. Kelber, *The Oral and the Written Gospel* (Philadelphia: Fortress Press, 1983). Against this hypothesis cf. Halverson (as in note 30), especially 191-193, and already Schweizer (as in note 30) 37-39, also 27-28 (4.3-4 with note 33), 41(7.2) and 49 (8.4).

89. The first appearance of the risen Lord probably took place in Galilee (cf. below pp. 78-79) and this caused Mark to include at 16:7 the instruction by the"young man"/angel to go thither.

90. The context of the saying is in Luke 13:28-30 and 13:34-35 Q, but it is very uncertain whether this is the original context, cf. Matt 8:11-12 and 23:37-39, and J. S. Kloppenborg, *Q-Parallels* (Sonoma: Polebridge, 1988), 158.

91. Cf. Fitzmyer (as in note 43), 1028-1030, for both alternatives.

92. Matthew connects it with 23:34-36/Luke 11:49-51 Q. If this were the context of Q, it might suggest that the Jerusalem saying was originally a word of Wisdom-Sophia (Luke 11:49 !). In this case, it could have been taken over from an earlier Jewish text. Or Jesus himself (or a Christian) could have formulated it on the background of sayings like Ben Sirach 24:10-11 ("in Zion"..."the beloved city.") This would neither prove nor disprove authenticity.

93. Crossan (as in note 16), 255-256; for his predecessors cf. R. Bultmann, *Die Geschichte der synoptischen Tradition* 6th ed. (Göttingen: Vandenhoeck & Ruprecht, 1964), 27, note 3. See also above pp. 50-51.

94. Fitzmyer (as in note 43), 785. Yet he adds that a modern preacher would scarcely tell his audience to be ready "to face the firing line or to strap themselves into an electric chair." But might he not speak of situations in which it could become necessary "to put one's head into the noose"?

95. Ibid. G. Schwarz, "Der Nachfolgespruch Markus 8.34bc Parr.," *NTS* 33, (1987): 255-265, even suggests an Aramaic term in this sense, which could have been understood also as pointing to the cross.

96. Also in 2 Clements 5:2-4 (quotation from the gospel of the Egyptians? cf. K. Aland, *Synopsis quattuor evangeliorum* Stuttgart: Bibelanstalt, 1964, 141, on Matt 10:16). Cf. also Matt 10:24/Luke 6:40 Q; Matt 10:28-36/Luke 12:4-9,51-56 Q (see below 57-62).

97. So even Lüdemann (as in note 26), 124. It is very unlikely that there ever arose a situation in the early church in which such strong opposition to Peter would have been expressed in this way. Gnostic polemics against him (cf. Lüdemann, 195-196) are of much later origin.

98. Though lacking in Matthew the verse might have belonged to Q, cf. Kloppenborg (as in note 90), 142.

99. See p. 40 and note 54.

100. According to Acts 12:2, only James was killed.

101. In the Hebrew Bible "many" often describes the totality (of Israel, for instance) without limiting the number, but without defining it mathematically either, as if no exceptions were possible.

102. On Is 53 cf. most recently O. Hofius, "Das vierte Gottesknechtlied in den Briefen des Neuen Testamentes," *NTS* 39, (1993): 414-437, though V. Hampel, *Menschensohn und historischer Jesus, ein Rätselwort als Schlüssel zum messianischen Selbstvertändnis Jesu,* (Neukirchen-Vluyn: Neukirchener, 1990), considers Mark 10:45 authentic, but not influenced by Is 53.

103. Cf. p.49 with note 70, also Marshall (as in note 63), 811: "The Markan passage is more semitic in style than Luke's form, but Luke's setting at table is more likely to be original."

104. Five times in Esther, once in Proverbs and once in 4 Maccabees.

105. Cf. above p. 26.

106. Fitzmyer (as in note 43), 1412-1415, votes for the priority of Mark 10:41-45, but the Lukan version could (with some later redactional changes removed) be "traced back in some form to the historical Jesus."

107. Cf. Justinus, *Apologia* I 66:3 "This is my body"/"This is my blood."

108. E. Schweizer, article "soma," ThWNT VII, 1056.

109. The latter is missing in some old manuscripts, probably left out by some copyists to avoid a second word about the cup (E. Schweizer, *The Good News according to Luke* (Atlanta: John Knox, 1984), 332.

110. This could be an earlier variant of Mark 14:25, but might equally well be a later expansion.

111. According to Mark 14:23 the disciples drink from the cup *before* Jesus interprets it as being his blood! On the problem of the tradition of the last supper see also my article "Body," in AncB Dictionary I, (1991), 769-770. My remarks concern misunderstandings, not (Roman-) Catholic doctrine of today.

112. Schürmann (as in note 86), 56-63.

113. Crossan (as in note 16), 361.

114. Schweizer (as in note 30), 55; Lüdemann (as in note 26), 57.

115. The first *and* last year of a period were counted at that time, as a rule.

116. In addition to the passages mentioned above on pp. 55-57, we may also compare Luke 13:32, which speaks explicitly of the end of Jesus' ministry: "I cast out demons and perform cures today and tomorrow and the third day I finish my course" (cf. John 9:4). Mark 2: 19b,20 does the same: "When the bridegroom is taken away (gospel of Thomas 104: "... comes out of the bride-chamber"!), then they will fast in that day" (on Friday?)—but this may be the post-Easter interpretation of an authentic word of Jesus in v. 19a: "Can the wedding guest fast while the bridegroom is with them?" (where "while" might suggest the limit of his presence). Mark 12:1-12 tells of the death of the "beloved son" within the parable; again, the authenticity of this parable, though it is also reported in the gospel of Thomas 65, is not beyond doubt.

117. Bultmann (as in note 5), 36, note 2, (originally p. 23, note 20).

118. See above pp. 21-23.

119. See pp. 26-27 and note 48.

120. See pp. 25-26.

121. See ibid., especially the Freudian interpretations of the psychiatrist on p. 27.

122. I do not maintain that this is necessarily an authentic word of Jesus; the veracity of this statement is not dependent on the question whether it was spoken by the historical Jesus.

123. E. Moltmann-Wendel [*eadem*/J. Moltmann, *Als Frau und Mann von Gott reden* (Kaiser-Taschenbuch, 1991), 111-117] speaks of the solidarity of the women with the dead Jesus. They do what the male disciples should have done, but did not do (Mark 10:43-44), they "serve" (Mark 1:31; 15:41; Luke 8:3). They render Jesus the last debt of honor and buy spices to anoint his corpse. Strangely enough, whereas for the male disciples the crucifixion was the dreadful shock, for the female disciples it was his resurrection (Mark 16:8), which deprived them of the opportunity to serve him.

124. No longer facing the danger of boasting spiritualists (as in 2 Cor 5:12 etc., still influencing Rom 6), but facing instead the dan-

ger of rigorism and legalism, Col 2:12 can say that as the readers have been buried with Christ in baptism, they also have been raised with him.

125. The contrasting interpretation of Rom 6:1-11 by Käsemann, *An die Römer*, HNT 8a, (1973) on the one hand, and by U. Wilckens, *Der Brief an die Römer*, EKK 6/1, (1978) on the other, is illuminating.

126. C. Breytenbach, *Versöhnung*, WMANT 60, (1989), and idem, "Versöhnung, Stellvertretung und Sühne; Semantische und traditionsgeschichtliche Bemerkungen am Beispiel der paulinischen Briefe," *NTS* 39, (1993): 59-79.

127. *Hilasterion* in Rom 3:25 is, perhaps, not the means of expiation, but describes merely Jesus as the place where expiation may be found. W. Schenk, "Sühnemittel" oder "Gnadenort," in: C. Mayer and others (ed.), *Nach den Anfängen fragen* (Festschrift G. Dautzenberg), Giessen, (1994), 553-567; but cf. D.C. Campbell, *The Rhetoric of Righteousness in Romans 3:21-26*, JSNTSup 65, (1992), 133. In Mark 10:45 *lytron* may merely mean "redemption' (but in 1 Peter 1:18 the original meaning is still alive).

128. Someone who has been freed from the life-long depression of guilt, may very well confess that Jesus Christ died as a sacrifice in order to redeem him or her. Another one, the course of whose life has totally changed because through Jesus new challenges and new joys have been given so that old interests and passions have faded out, may equally well confess that Jesus had to pay the ransom to liberate him or her for a new life. A man I know who has been tortured in a South American torture cellar, told us that the only thought that was still alive in him was that Jesus had also been where he was then; hence, he spoke in terms of the solidarity of his brother Jesus with him, in order to confess the truth.

CHAPTER V

129. Cf. pp. 25 and 62-63 with note 117.

130. Niederwimmer, (as in note 35), especially 42-48.

131. Cf. p. 5 and note 5.

132. Bultmann (as in note 5), 31 (originally on p. 16). Cf. K. Barth, in *Kerygma und Mythos* (as in note 6), II 102-109 (= *Kirchliche Dogmatik* III/2, 531-537), especially p.108. Barth speaks of the story of the resurrection of Jesus in the form of a "Sage" or "Legende," i.e. of a fact not to be verified by the tools of the historian; but he insists that it has really happened, as many other facts of this kind have done so (pp.106-107).

133. Cf. note 26. For the following, see my article "Resurrection" in *A New Handbook of Christian Theology*, (Nashville TN:

Abingdon, 1992), 402-408, and my essay "Resurrection: Fact or Illusion?" in *Horizons in Biblical Theology*, Pittsburgh Theological Seminary, I, (1979): 137-159.

134. Cf. p. 55 and note 89.

135. Acts 2:1, also Lüdemann (as in note 26), 130 and 210-211.

136. "Crucified—buried ('see the place where they laid him')—risen—to be seen by his disciples and Peter" like 1 Cor 15:3-5! It is still a possibility to be considered, though, that some story or stories of Jesus appearing to his disciples have been lost or torn away from a very early copy of Mark's gospel. For Q cf. pp. 11-12.

137. For instance, 1 Thess 5: 10: "who died for us."

138. Rom 8:11: (God) "who raised Jesus from the dead." Cf. 1 Cor 6: 14; 2 Cor 4:14.

139. Rom 14:9: "Christ died and lived again," cf. Rom 4:25. In a more active way, which might be of a later origin, Christ's act is described as "he gave himself for me" (Gal 2:20) or "Jesus died and rose again" (1 Thess 4:14; together with Rom 14:9, these are the only passages in which Paul uses the verb "to rise" for Jesus). Cf. W. Popkes, *Christus traditus. Eine Untersuchung zum Begriff der Dahingabe im Neuen Testament*, AThANT 49, (1967).

140. "God sent forth his son..." (Gal 4:4). Cf. Rom 8:3; John 3:16,17; 1 John 4:9, always connected with the idea of his redeeming death (cf. Gal 4:5 with 3:13; "for sin" in Rom 8:3; the context of John 3:14-15 and 1 John 4:10). See E. Schweizer, "What Do We Really Mean When We Say 'God sent his son...'?" *in: Faith and History*, (Festschrift P. W. Meyer) (Atlanta: Scholars Press, 1990), 298-312.

141. "Christ Jesus...who is at the right hand of God" (Rom 8:34). "No one can say 'Jesus is Lord' except by the Holy Spirit" (1 Cor 12:3).

142. Phil 2:11 probably understood this from the beginning of the tradition as the eschatological triumph at the parousia (which is certainly Paul's own understanding: Rom 14:11), cf. O. Hofius, *Der Christushymnus Phil 2,6-11*, WUNT 17, (1976), 33-34, 41-45, 67-74, 102. The parousia is mentioned in the formula of 1 Thess 1:10. Otherwise, it appears more often in exclamations and prayers: "maranatha" (1 Cor 16:22). It is the object of the hope of the church, not a saving event to be confessed in a credal formula.

143. In 1960 I already tried to deal with the history of these traditions in *Lordship and Discipleship* (London: SCM), especially 49-67.

144. Cf. p. 61.

145. The perfect tense emphasizes that this has happened once and that the result of the event is still present.

146. "The twelve" is obviously a traditional term, which appears only here in Paul's letters; actually there were eleven (Matt 28:

16 par.).

147. Cf. W. Michaelis, "horao," ThWNT V 333, and Lüdemann (as in note 26), 71.

148. Michaelis, ibid.

149. In contrast to Lüdemann, 113-115, I do not think that Luke 5:1-11 was originally an Easter story (cf. John 21:1-16), because the marks of these stories are lacking (the disciples' doubts and their conquest, a commission of the disciples and the vanishing of Jesus), whereas miracles (like the marvelous fishing story), actually competing with the miracle of the resurrection, do not belong to the Easter stories. See Schweizer, (as in note 109), 102-103.

150. Compare Matt 28:9; John 20:14-17, and below pp. 79-80 and 82-84.

151. Written in the first half of the second century? It is quoted by Hieronymus, cf. Lüdemann (as in note 26), 139-141.

152. Junia is a female first name; there is no male name Junia or Junias (both forms possible in Rom 16:7). Cf. R.S. Cervin, "A Note Regarding the name 'Junia(s)' in Romans 16.7," *NTS* 40, (1994): 464-470. For further literature cf. the most recent commentaries, for instance J. Edwards, *Romans* (Peabody: Hendrickson, 1991), 355 and 363. According to Phil 4:3 two other women "have labored side by side with me (Paul) in the (proclamation of the) gospel."

153. Of course, this does not necessarily mean that they have really done so or indicate in what way they have done so (see pp. 78-85). But it does mean that the list cannot be dismissed as a list of mere formulas of legitimation (as suggests R. Pesch, "Materialien und Bemerkungen zu Entstehung und Sinn des Osterglaubens," in: A. Vögtle/ R. Pesch, *Wie kam es zum Osterglauben* ? ppb (1975), 156; thereby legitimizing a teacher whose preaching caused ecstatic experiences but without claiming an original vision of the risen Lord. Similarly U. Wilckens, *Auferstehung,ThTh* 4, (1970): 25-26; H. P. Hasenfratz, *Die Rede von der Auferstehung Christi, FThL* 10, (1975): 154-155, and still yet Crossan (as in note 16), 410-411. Some competition for leadership might be mirrored in the parallel phrases "to Peter, then to the twelve" and "to James, then to all the apostles," though.

154. Acts 22:6-11; 26:12-18 are, by and large, secondary to Acts 9:3-9: Lüdemann (as in note 26), 84-87.

155. It must have been the first for Matthew, since "some doubted," which would be impossible after what Luke 24 or John 20 tell. (Mark and) Matthew report no other appearance.

156. If one explains the appearances as mere intrapsychic experiences, simultaneous appearances are improbable, because the first one must cause others, and therefore the second and third and the following experiences are dependent on the knowledge of some former experiences; compare p. 80 and Lüdemann (as in note 26), 39, to F. Bovon.

157. Was it in the evening (which is for a Jew the beginning of the new day), as Matt 28:1 says (cf., for instance my *Good News according to Matthew* (Atlanta: John Knox 1975/London: SPCK, 1976), 523, or in the morning before or at sunrise? The difference between Matthew and the other gospels may be due to different translations of an original Aramaic source: J. M. Winger, "When Did the Women Visit the Tomb?" *NTS* 40, (1994), 284-288.

158. Luke 24:12 (probably original in Luke's text) and 24:24 tell of a visit of Peter (v.12) or of "some of us" (v.24) at the tomb, but *after* the angels spoke to the women.

159. Lüdemann (as in note 26), 147-148. Compare also note 157 above. Mark 16:9-20 is a later appendix, not belonging to the original gospel.

160. L. Oberlinner, "Die Verkündigung der Auferweckung Jesu im geöffneten und leeren Grab." *ZNW* 73, (1982): 159-182, shows that the tomb being *open* provides even more difficulties than its having been *empty*.

161. Lüdemann (as in note 26), 126-128.

162. Ibid. 136-138.

163. Early predecessors proposing this theory include: P. W. Schmiedel, EB (c) IV (1903), 4039-4086; A. Meyer, *Die Auferstehung Christi* (1905), 217-315, in: P. Hoffmann (ed.), *Zur neutestamentlichen Ueberlieferung von der Auferstehung Jesu*, WdF 522, (1988), 62-67 (Einführung, by the editor); literature from 1770 up to 1986 on pp. 453-483. Some major works on the 19th century are discussed in Lüdemann, 77-83.

164. Gal 1:15-16; 1 Cor 9:1; Acts 9:4-6, cf. 26:16-18.

165. Michaelis (as in note 147), 355-357.

166. G. Sellin, "Hauptprobleme des ersten Korintherbriefes," ANRW 25.4, (1987), 3025. Cf. also Lüdemann (as in note 26), 198-199.

167. He uses the term *optasiai* ("visions"). The genitive "of the Lord" is not genitivus objectivus, but auctoris (given by the Lord). The text may presuppose some seeing (not of the Lord), but Paul actually mentions only "*hearing* things that cannot be told."

168. G. Lohfink, *Die Himmelfahrt Jesu*, (Munich: Kösel, 1971), 111-146, though these traditions show also their dependence on Acts 1. For a different dating of the ascension see Luke 24:51 (the longer text probably being original) and John 20:17.

169. Lüdemann (as in note 26), 131-138.

170. Ibid., 152-153: especially E. Bickermann. Lüdemann also brings forward Hellenistic parallels.

171. The same might be true of the original Jewish-Christian formula in Rom 1:4, if it was Paul who added "by his resurrection from the dead." Compare also Acts 3:21. In John, the exaltation of Jesus to the cross (3:13-14; 12:32-34) influences also the use of this term in

6:62.

172. But this could also be due to the influence of Hosea 6:2.

173. "Die Erscheinung des auferstandenen Christus" (1957) in: Hoffmann (as in note 163), 311, quoted by Lüdemann (as in note 26), 191. "The appearances of the Risen Christ," in C. H. Dodd, *More New Testament Studies* (Manchester: University Press, 1968), 115 (originally in *Studies in the Gospels. Essays in Memory of R. H. Lightfoot,* Blackwell 1957).

174. S. Heine, in Lüdemann, 196.

175. It goes without saying that this does not say that Jesus was lifted up from the earth to a heaven above the earth, but that he has been transferred into another dimension of life.

176. We accept parapsychological facts: that a watch stops or a clock falls from the wall when a person dies (as happened with my sister-in-law), because we admit there are influences about which we know very little or nothing. I do not contend that the traces of the resurrection of Jesus were parapsychological facts, because then they would be defined as powerful influences emanating from a dying person. But I ask: why are we so ready to accept such facts yet afraid of the thought that God, on a totally different level, might move by his word and spirit—not merely human thoughts and emotions—but also physical objects? Is this so different from, for instance, nerves being relaxed or ulcers healed?

177. A saying of Martin Luther is often retold (I cannot guarantee its authenticity) that he had many more experiences of God in his youth than in later life and that he did not see this as a regression, but as progress, because he had learnt in the meantime to trust the word of God without forcing God to create a special miracle, before he, Martin Luther, would listen and do what God wanted from him.

178. Crossan (as in note 16), 248-249.

179. Lüdemann (as in note 26), 97: 1 Enoch 71:5; Apocalypsis Esrae 1:2-9 (in the context of 1:1 and 1:10-13); Bill. III 531; Mohammed in H. Windisch, *Der zweite Korintherbrief,* KEK VI, 1970 (=1924) 370, note 2. A medieval example seems to be Niklaus von Flüe, who tells of one of his visions: "ein mensch brach den schlaf durch gozwillen und durch sine lides willen...," but it is not quite clear whether this is an autograph (P. A. Wagner, in: *Der Geschichtsfreund* 83, (1928), 110,112).

180. Cf. note 76. It was only in the church that the figure of the witness became that of the judge. How easily this happens can be seen by comparing Rom 14:10 with 2 Cor 5:10 ("the judgment seat of God/of Christ") or even within 1 Cor 4:4-5 ("*It is the Lord* who judges me...the Lord comes, who will bring to light the things that are hidden in darkness and will disclose the purposes of the heart; then every man will receive his recommendation from God").

181. Cf. above p. 55.

182. Cf. above pp. 51-52.

183. Cf. the famous dictum of E. Käsemann that apocalypticism is the mother (I suggested: the midwife) of Christian theology ("Zum Thema der urchristlichen Apokalyptik," in: idem, *Exegetische Versuche und Besinnungen,* vol. II (Göttingen: Vandenhoeck & Ruprecht, 1964,) 130-131, and other contributions that are critically reviewed by G. Klein, "Eschatologie," TRE X, 274-275.

184. I have also interpreted this story in *Jesus Christ,* (as in note 11), 52-55.

CHAPTER VI

185. Boldern-Texte, Männedorf/Switzerland: Boldern, May 2, 1994.

186. The category of "motivation" may not suffice (cf. pp. 3 and 4-5), but there is no doubt that Bultmann thought of an "objective" act of God.

187. At around ninety years of age, Bultmann wrote to me on a post-card as a postscript: "All is grace, nothing but grace."

188. Including some unconscious channels of influence.

189. The phrase (without an emphatic "the") is to be found in E. Schillebeeckx, *Jesus. Die Geschichte von einem Lebenden,* 7th edition, (Freiburg: Herder, 1980), 555 (title); E. Jüngel, *Gott als Geheimnis der Welt,* 2nd edition (Tübingen: Mohr, 1977), 491, 495; L. E. Keck, *A Future for the Historical Jesus* (Philadelphia: Fortress, 1982), 35, 174-175; and Sölle, (as in note 11), 183.

190. Suppose that when my father died I was twenty years old, but my younger brother had just been born. I would then have known my father, whilst my younger brother would not, but I would never think that I would necessarily be the better son of my father than my brother!

191. This may well be due to appalling pastoral instruction, or to the terrifying threats of parents, or to "Christian" friends that let them down!

192. When defining what the function of Biblical or dogmatic statements are, I often use the picture of a highway, the guard rails and lines of which—on the left and on the right—prevent me from driving into an abyss or onto the lane with the traffic coming in the other direction. They may save my life more than once. But if I thought of driving on the lines (or even the guard rails!) themselves, a catastrophe would be certain. Rather, I should drive *between* the lines and should decide whether I want to do so slowly and stay behind the other cars, or accelerate and overtake. This is up to me to do in full freedom. It would not help either, simply to stay close to the first lines so as to be quite sure never to cross over, because in this case I would never reach my desti-

nation. Moreover, the lines are following one another in continuation, but where I am driving just now they are not the same lines as the lines where I started my drive. Similarly the statements within the New Testament and throughout the centuries of the later church stay in some sort of continuation, if they are good statements, but they are never literally the same, because in another time and situation literal repetition might say the contrary of what it had originally intended (cf. pp. 35-40).

INDEX

Selected Biblical Passages
(numbers refer to *pages*)

INDEX

Authors
(Numbers refer to *notes*)